# Daughters of Dakota

Schooled in Privation
German, German-Russian and Scandinavian
Immigrants in South Dakota

edited by
Sally Roesch Wagner

Volume IV

GFWC of SD/DOD
Box 349
Yankton, SD 57078

Copyright © 1991 by Sally Roesch Wagner.
All rights reserved. Printed in the United States.

ISBN 1-880589-04-4 (Vol. IV)
ISBN 1-880589-00-1 (Set)

The cover photo is of Rosina Treftz Roesch. The other photographs, chosen by LaVera Rose, are from the Pioneer Daughters collection of the General Federation of Women's Clubs of South Dakota. The collection is housed in the South Dakota Historical Society.

DAUGHTERS OF DAKOTA
P.O. Box 349
Yankton, SD 57078

*To my father*
*Frederich*
*in memory of his mother*

# TABLE OF CONTENTS

Introduction .................................................................................... vii

The Germans from Russia ............................................................ 1
Rosina Treftz Roesch; Edmunds County, 1898 ...................... 6
Susana Weidner Schamber; Yankton County, 1875 ............... 15
Dorothea Bietz; Hutchinson and Douglas Counties, 1879 ..... 19
Elizabeth Bauder Max; Bon Homme County, 1873 ................ 21
Eva Kliewer Tieszen; Turner County, 1874 ............................ 23
Huether Bitz Orth; McPherson County, Before 1889 ............. 25

The Germans
Emily Hoffmann Baumgarten; Edmunds County, 1885 ......... 27
Amalia Oppenheimer Colman; Lawrence County, 1877 ........ 32
Charlotte Catharina Reitman Bottcher; Hyde County, 1883 ... 35
Wilhemeina Klipstine Yada Haack; Codington County, 1879 .. 40
Rosina Schoessler; Davison County, 1882 ............................. 45
Anna Katherina Rosenmeier Stuempge; Turner County, 1879. 47
Anna Kretchmer Rother; Beadle County, 1889 ...................... 52

Scandinavians ............................................................................... 56
The Norwegians
Susanna Larsen Bergh; Brown County, 1881 ......................... 59
Nellie Proper Beachem Hunstad; Brown County, 1880 ......... 63
Marie Holstad; Brown County, 1893 ....................................... 66
Ingeborg Aaker Simons; Minnehaha County, 1877 ................ 68
Kristianna Sigdestad Olson; Day County, 1889 ..................... 81
Rasmene Vanelven Warren and Anna Warren Peart;
  Moody County, 1878 ............................................................. 85
Kristina Eidsness Tollefson: Lincoln County, 1888 ............... 98
Ingeborg E. Wangen Buene; Brown County, 1883 ................ 100
Margret Hjelmeland Knutson; Aurora County, 1882 ............ 104
Kristianna Ortness Trygstad; Brookings County, 1869 ......... 109

The Swedes
    Hilma Rudine Olson; Hyde County, 1883 ...................................115
    Kristina J. Carlson Johnson; Hyde County, 1887 ....................120
    Mathilda Andersdotter Berg; Grant County, 1881 ....................143

The Lone Dane
    Marie Christensen Johnson; Clay County, 1870 ........................146

Midwives and a Doctor ..........................................................................149

Accounts of the Trip Over .....................................................................155

# INTRODUCTION

Nearly half of all of us living in the United States today are related to people who immigrated here from Europe between 1880 and 1920. During those four peak decades over twenty million people pulled up their roots and replanted them with the hope of a better life in the United States.
White settlement in Dakota Territory began in earnest during the "Great Dakota Boom" from 1870-1880. The population exploded by 734 percent during that time, and another 255 percent during the next decade. The majority of immigrants were Scandinavians, Germans and Germans from Russia. These stories focus on those who came before the turn of the century to the land east of the Missouri river, land which had been acquired for white settlement from the Sioux nation under the Treaty of 1868.
There were differences by ethnicity, but many experiences in the "new country" were shared by all these immigrant groups. They all feared the Indians, but none had any problems with them. They all suffered equally from droughts, blizzards, prairie fires and grasshoppers.
They came because the land was free, conditions were bad in the old country, land and railroad agents enticed them with mouth-watering propaganda, and friends and relatives who had already come to Dakota encouraged them to do likewise. Welcomed into the two-room shanties of the families who had arrived earlier, the newcomers located land and constructed temporary housing.
Nothing was easy. The land, which was their salvation, also stole their spirits. They never triumphed over nature. If they were lucky, it was a draw. Schools were built immediately. Their children must be educated at all costs; that education ripped them from their cultural moorings. American was best and the old ways were buried in attics. English was the bridge to the new world, but their native language carried the memory of who they were. At every turn, they were pulled between the old country and the new. At best,

the dynamic tension propelled their families into a success beyond their wildest dreams. Sometimes it stretched them to the breaking point.

Religion sustained these women. It was the rock on which they grounded themselves. They helped each other adjust to the strangeness, midwived each other's births, and sometimes buried each other. Often they married, not for love, but because a young man they hardly knew had come back home looking for a wife. They birthed many babies, and many died, and the new ones who came were given the names of those who never made it past infancy with the hope that perhaps this time the name would survive.

They knew nothing of the cult of domesticity occupied by the tea-cup ladies of the native-born, affluent white world they'd come to, these women who picked up the gang plow, as they always had. They worked alongside their husband in the field, and without him, if he died.

"Savages," the terror they had been told to dread, turned out to be darker-skinned counterparts of themselves, working hard to survive. In story after story, these women describe the "Indian scare" they experienced in December 1890. Each one in turn says there was nothing to the reports of an Indian uprising. But not one knew about the murder by the military of over 300 Lakota at Wounded Knee. These women also use the language of the time and refer to American Indian women as "squaws," not knowing the disrespectful and insulting meaning of the term.

A word about editing. The "melting pot" method of assimilation furiously boiled away cultural diversity in custom and language; it was even against the law in South Dakota for a time to use any language but English in public. Still, the patterns of grammar persisted after the mother tongue had been all but silenced. The voices of these immigrant women, even when put down by daughters who never knew the old country, have a richness of ethnic and regional flavor that I have worked hard not to homogenize.

Editing has been light. Grammar, punctuation and spelling have been left intact when unusual forms seemed to represent ethnic styles. Genealogical information has been removed, since any interested reader can obtain the original, unedited stories from the South Dakota Historical Society.

When words that might not have been used by the author of the story were added for clarity, they have been bracketed.

"She/I was born..." began almost every single one of these stories, and that universal opening line has been kept.

Special thanks to Anne Roesch Larson, Helen Bergh, Dr. Harry Delker, Julie Davies and LaVera Rose for their help with this volume.

## COUNTY MAP FOR THE STATE OF SOUTH DAKOTA

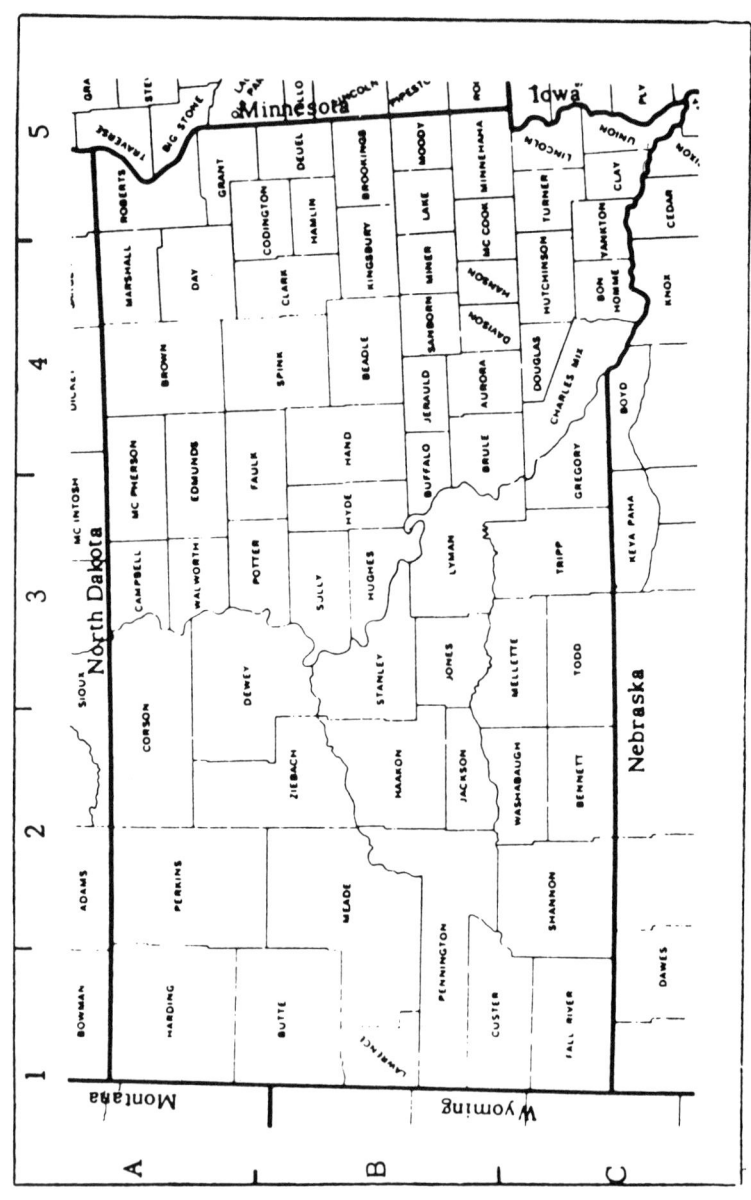

# THE GERMANS FROM RUSSIA

"I like planting, Sally," my seven year old city grandson exclaims as he runs out the door of my lake cabin with his second handful of seed packets. "Now that I know how to do it, I love it." I wonder if it might be congenital, this love of making things grow. Last summer my father and I experimented with an Indian garden: corn, beans and squash in a mound, where Michael is sowing marigold and sunflower seeds today. My Aunt Annie's garden yearly brings forth an abundance of everything for the table, and the scraps return to the garden in a never-ending cycle. The love of farming goes back far in our family.

My ancestors lived in a crowded, war-torn Germany two centuries ago. Young men were drafted into the army, where they wasted their best years fighting the endless wars of the fatherland. Land was scarce; people were poor.

So when Catherine, Empress of Russia, (herself of German descent) published a manifesto in German papers in 1763, enticing "unser Leute" (our people) to leave their rich, if small, farmlands in Germany, she sweetened the pot because they were known to be such fine farmers. After five centuries of fighting to regain control of their land from the Mongols, the Russians had finally restored their Volga steppes. Catherine wanted the Germans to cultivate this vast untilled land and introduce their superior agricultural methods to the area. Free land – 162 acres of it, she promised them, plus a low-interest loan of 250-300 rubles to get them started and rations until their first harvest. Beyond that, they would be able to set up their own churches, schools and local governments. And perhaps most importantly, the young men would be exempted forever from military service. Northern Germans responded in droves.

The experiment in German colonists proved so successful that when Russia pushed the Turks out of the Ukraine and gained control of the Black Sea area, Catherine's grandson issued a second decree forty years later. This one was directed at the overcrowded Southern Germans.

It was Alexander I's call on February 22, 1804 for "a limited number of such immigrants as can serve as models for agricultural occupations and handicrafts" that brought Michael's ancestors from the state of Wurttemberg to the village of Glueckstahl, ninety miles from Odessa. Here they, along with 180 other colonies, came to be known as the Schwartzmeerdeutsche (Black Sea Germans). Superior agriculturalists and artisans, they set-up model villages, neat and orderly, and turned Russia into the bread basket of the world.

They were *too* good, family tradition taught me, and eventually the 100,000 German-Russian farmers roused the jealousy of the local Russians, who resented these aloof colonists who kept to themselves, speaking their own language, practicing their own religion and customs, and generally marrying only their own kind. Why should they be excused from the responsibility of protecting their country?

Eventually the angry Russians pressured Czar Alexander II to revoke the special rights and privileges granted the German colonists, and after the sweeping Codex of the Colonists on June 4, 1871, the German-Russians began looking for a new home. Having lost their local self-government, they found themselves without judicial rights and prey to roving gangs of thieves, from whom there was no recourse in the Russian judicial system. Beyond this, the Schwartzmeerdeutsche found especially unacceptable the removal of their exemption from military service.

"We were the original draft dodgers," my Uncle John laughed. He was telling how the hired man hid under the hired girl's skirts in the wagon when the Roesch family left their Glueckstahl home for America. With the local authorities waiting to draft him into the army, this young man sneaked out of the country.

I asked my father once why the only picture of his whole family looked so gloomy. It was taken on the eve of Uncle John's departure to World War I, my dad explained, and just as the folks in the old country dreaded conscription into the Czar's army, because those who went off to Siberia seldom returned, just so the family feared that they would never see Johann again.

"I'll never forget the day I left for camp," my Uncle John reminisced. "I woke up about daylight and there's dad standing beside the bed crying. He said, 'On account of you I left Russia, so you wouldn't have to serve in the army, and here we are.' " "Times change," John shrugged. "I have two boys and they both had their hitch and they don't think nothin' of it."

But I'm getting ahead of myself. At the same time that they were being pushed out of Russia, my grandparents were being drawn to America, where the Homestead Act of 1862 made 160 acres of free land available to anyone willing to work it. The German-Russians were courted, actually, by agents for the U.S. railroads, the new land barons of America, who had received vast land holdings in exchange for laying track the length of the country. The railroads wanted to sell this land and, more importantly, they needed farmers who would raise large crops and pay the large sums the railroads charged for hauling their produce to market.

Dakota Territory established a Bureau of Immigration, while real estate and business interests joined forces with steamship companies to fund the propaganda which the agents distributed. Throughout the Russian steppes (and much of Europe) they proclaimed the virtues of the Great untapped Plains, hoping that these tried-and-true agricultural wizards could dispel the prevalent myth about the unsuitability of the region (the Great American Desert, it was called) for farming.

And so the second massive immigration of unser Leute began in 1873, when an advance party of five Lutheran Germans from Russia made it to Yankton, the capitol of Dakota Territory, the end-station of a newly completed railroad. Part of a larger party of twelve delegates who had scoured Michigan, Illinois and Wisconsin searching for available land on which to establish isolated settlements, these Dakota scouts found not only available homestead land, but also the same black soil and steppes they had left in Russia. By year's end 500 of my people had settled in Yankton county; two years later, there were 5,000 German-Russians in Dakota. They brought with them the Turkey Red hard wheat which became the foundation of America's wheat farming.

Once again, with adequate rainfall on their side, the Germans from Russia proved their green thumbs and brought forth the bumper crops that the boomers pointed to with pride in enticing additional settlers.

They came, not one at a time, but by families and villages, and they named their settlements after the places they had come from: Odessa, Worms, Petersburg, Friedenstal, so that you can find families from Kassel, South Dakota, who trace their ancestry back to Kassel in the old country. The settlers spread out into available land to the north and west, filling the counties of Yankton, Bon Homme, Hutchinson and Douglas, and then, when they'd taken all available lands there, using the old settlements as bases, they began to homestead west and northwest of Ipswich.

The German-Russian village of my grandparents, Glueckstahl, relocated around Hosmer and Bowdle. A township in McPherson County, right next to nearby Eureka, is named Glueckstahl. Eureka, the final stop on the railroad, became another settlement base. A tribute to the farming genius of my people, by 1892 Eureka became known as the wheat capitol, the largest inland wheat-shipping point in the world.

Again the settlers spread out as more and more of them arrived, and by the time South Dakota became a state in 1889, Edmunds, McPherson, Campbell and Walworth counties were heavily populated with German-Russians from the Black Sea steppes. Even today this area of Edmunds and McPherson counties: Java, Roscoe, etc., is largely German-speaking. "Bowdle-out" non-German/Russians mimic the language patterns of the population.

When the drought years drove the Easterners back home during the late 1880's, it opened more land for incoming immigrants. As more Indian land was taken for white settlement, Germans from Russia moved into it, settling in Gregory and Tripp counties after the turn of the century. The 1920 census showed over 300,000 Germans from Russia settled all over the United States; one-tenth of them, the third largest percentage, in South Dakota.

The area around Hosmer and Eureka had received German immigrants from Russia for over fourteen years before my grandparents, the Roeschs, arrived in 1898 to stay with relatives until they bought the Regan-Hooper ranch five miles north of Roscoe. Across the road my grandfather filed a homestead claim.

"Aller anfang est schwer," all beginnings are hard, my father wrote to me when I left my daughter and my home for graduate school, and it is a truism that runs deep in our genetic knowledge.

My grandfather hadn't counted on the rocks. Debris of a receding glacier millennia before, they dotted the semi-arid landscape, and became the herculean challenge of a growing "gemeinde" (community) of little Roeschs. Along with the rocks, which they stacked in mounds, my aunts and uncles gathered buffalo bones, which they took by the wagonload to Roscoe, and were paid by the ton for this echo of the recently destroyed buffalo culture. The bones were shipped East on the railroad, where they were ground into fertilizer and returned, at a much higher price, to the farmers.

Gopher tails brought one cent apiece, "a pretty good income in those days," my Uncle Ed claims. They used traps only. They couldn't shoot because they didn't have ammunition.

"An area where climatic conditions, unfavorable to a permanent agricultural economy, recur with irregular persistency" wrote the geographer, C. Warren Thornthwaite. The local banker took my grandfather aside and confided that the land wasn't suitable for farming, and he should raise cattle instead. My grandfather did. It was also very clear that a much larger land base than the 160 acres allotted to homesteaders was necessary to survive.

SOME SOURCES:
Harry A. Delker, *The Bertsch Book — 222 Years.* Aberdeen, South Dakota: 1986.
John Edward Pfeiffer, "The German-Russians and Their Immigration to South Dakota," *Report and Historical Collections* XXXV (1970).
Herbert S. Schell, *History of South Dakota*, Lincoln, NE: University of Nebraska Press, 1975.
*Germans from Russia Heritage Society*, 1008 East Central Avenue, Bismarck, ND 58501.

# Rosina Treftz Roesch
## Edmunds County
## 1898

I remember most of all her hands, thick and broad, gnarled like two tree stumps. "She baked fifteen loaves of bread a week," my Aunt Marie told me, "kneaded it all by hand—and her right arm was sort of deformed from this. The bread always raised beautifully; I never knew of a failure."

Rosina Treftz Roesch, my grandmother, was born in Glueckstahl, Russia in 1869 to John and Barbara Koerner Treftz. "Treftz nicht immer," her teacher told her.

I would be sitting at her feet in the upstairs bedroom, where she stayed with us part of the time during my childhood. Back and forth in her rocking chair, combing her long, black-streaked gray hair, she would laugh anew as she repeated the story for the umpteenth time. My eyes were riveted on her surprisingly agile fingers, holding the tortoise shell rounded comb like a small mouse in her ham of a hand, deftly drawing teeth so fine and thinly-spaced that they seemed impenetrable, through her thin hair. Then she would quickly weave a short strand of black material into a braid on either side. Bringing them around in back of her head, she tied the material together and hid it, then caught the braids on either side with two large bone hair pins. Her never idle hands picked up her knitting.

Laughing over earlier times as her fingers flicked back and forth, the crochet hooks my Uncle Ed had whittled for her circling the growing outline of the small rug she made, each day a new one, out of four skeins of yarn. Everybody got a rug when they came to visit her, and still there were cabinets full of them when she died. One of mine finally fell to pieces from wear and washing; the other two warm my feet in front of the reading chair in my study.

Her stories were seldom in English, most of the time she spoke in the "low" German that my people speak. Explained to me as describing the Southern part of Germany where we originated, I knew better. The "High" German of scholars and books was certainly loftier, and not geographically.

"Treftz nicht immer," she'd laugh, and while I couldn't speak the language, I knew the story well. Her name meant "catch it," and her teacher teased that she didn't always "catch it" when she wasn't paying attention.

This woman who had known sorrow that would strike a person dead, could laugh. And did. The humor I grew up around bubbled out of the unbearable hardness of life, and transcended it. "Besser a louse in kraut, als kein fleisch." "Rather a louse in the cabbage, than no meat at all."

When a neighboring farmhouse burned down, Uncle Jake solemnly declared, "I think it was friction on the mortgage." When his own service station went under, he shrugged it off with, "I was selling Gas for Less, but he never showed up." Driving a load of grain to market, Jacob hit a soft spot in the road and over went the truck. As he crawled out through the door, my uncle hollered to his companion, "Could you get the grease gun? I just found a zerk I've never been able to reach." None of the family smoked. "If the lord would have wanted you to smoke, he would have given you a chimney on your head," they say. My father repeats these stories with the frequency and relish with which his mother remembered "Treftz nicht immer." No matter how bad times get, something mournfully funny flowers through.

When I was quite small and sitting on her lap, Grandma Roesch's big hands would encircle my small ones, bringing them together in eye-blinking rhythmic claps, as she taught me:

> Backe, backe Kuchen,
> der Backer hat gerufen;
> Wer will guten Kuchen backen,
> der muss haben sieben Sachen –
> Eier und Salz, Butter und Schmalz,
> Milch und Mehl,
> Safrich macht den Kuchen gehl.
>   Kuchen gehl.
>   Kuchen gehl.

The village of Glueckstahl, Russia around 1890. The woman in the photo is Fredericka Treftz Jundt, oldest sister of Rosina Treftz Roesch. The building to the left is the church, the one next to it is the school, and the visible corner in the far right was the Roesch home.

Bake-a, bake-a cake,
the baker has declared;
If you want to bake good cake,
seven items you must take—
eggs and salt, lard and butter,
milk and flour,
saffron gives the yellow color.

And up would go our hands with "Kuchen gehl, Kuchen gehl."

Her father died when she was eight, but she never talked about that, or how hard times must have become for her and her four sisters, Karolina, Fredricka, Christiana and Kathrina.

Grandpa Roesch did. Orphaned at the age of seven, his sister took him in. He was hungry, he told his children, so hungry that he would go from house to house and eat the crumbs of bread that the women swept out their doors. "To this day," my Aunt Annie told me, "if I'm having company and somebody will put a piece of bread in the wastebasket, it'll make me shudder. I would never think of putting any bread in the wastebasket. Throw it to the birds." And I, only two generations removed from this gnawing hunger, understand why I grew up believing that "Waste not, want not" was the first commandment, and compulsively recycle leftovers into soup. It is almost a sacred trust, to carry the memory of that want.

Glueckstahl was "like the county seat," Uncle John told me. Eighty years later, he remembered the big walnut tree right on the corner of the house, the church, school and courthouse directly across the road, and the board fences around each yard. With hard work, Rosina and Frederich had made a good life for themselves. "They had beautiful land," my father explained. "They owned it, and were financially independent."

Fourteen babies were born to Rosina; five of them never made it through childhood. Two died unnamed at birth. Rosa, her first child, died at the age of two when her second baby was only a month old. Eva, the third, died of brain fever when she was eight days old. But it was the death of Frederich, the pious four year old, of which she could never speak without weeping.

"I am not going to the new country," he seriously told his parents. They humored him; of course he was. They had their passport with his name listed, and the letter from Rev. Schrenk, who had baptized, confirmed and married them, recommending the Roeschs to their new church in America with his farewell, "We regret the departure of this fine family from our Congregation. Your many Christians in this Assembly and from all of Lucky Valley are saddened by your departure." Feverishly the family worked to get everything ready, and to say their goodbyes.

Frederich got sick thirteen days before their scheduled departure date; he died of "hern entsentung," or brain infection, *ensephilitis*, three days before they left their home. "My parents left behind an open grave," my father wrote.

My grandmother never recovered from that shock. Long after they'd been in America, "when German people came to the house, before long she'd be telling this again and she'd be shedding tears along with them," my father told me. "Father would turn his back, cover his face, and I can still see his shoulders quiver." "They did not cry," Aunt Annie corrects, "they wept."

Grandma Roesch left a part of her spirit buried in that coffin, I think. As her next babies were born in America, she gave them the names of her dead children. First Rose, then Eva, and finally my father, Frederich, born four years after the death of her first Frederich. "Being the First Son born in America, I was given the name of my departed brother," my father wrote. In a patriarchal order, that meant he took on the responsibility of the namesake, the first born son, the family leader.

Religion sustained my grandmother. Daily bible-reading led to teaching all the children to read from the bible before they started off to school. April 1 was always remembered as the day she was confirmed. In later years she waited each week for the arrival of the Congregational *Der Kirchenbote*, carefully reading each article and obituary. When she died, her obituary was printed in the magazine.

Grandma Roesch had a strong sense of what was acceptable and what wasn't, based on her religious beliefs. Radio was ok, but movies were sinful. Her children, having grown up in a different world, didn't share all her beliefs, and wanted her to experience what they found enjoyable. Despite her objections, my Aunt Marie insisted that her mother accompany her to a movie. They got as far as the lobby, where my Grandma sat down in the middle of the floor and refused to budge. She died in 1954, never having seen the inside of a movie theatre.

Many of these immigrant German from Russia women never learned to speak English. They didn't need to. The women in Eureka, for example, were able to shop, worship, and visit with friends without ever leaving their native language. My grandmother was more isolated, and she learned to speak English from the teachers that roomed and boarded with the family. She could visit with her English-speaking neighbors in their tongue, although she never learned to write English.

My grandfather Frederich had two sisters and a stepsister and Rosina had one sister in the new country; that was all. They knew they would never see the rest of their families again. It was this isolation that was the hardest on her, and the other pioneer women, no matter where they came from. My grandmother had come from a village where family and friends were a hop, skip and a jump away. The men went out from the village to work in the fields during the day, and the women had each other for companionship.

In the new country she was deeply alone, in a social sense. Neighbors were culturally and geographically distant where 160 acres and often an alien heritage separated each family unit. "It was reported that the Insane Asylum at Yankton was filled with women who had been bereft of reason by the monotony and wretchedness of the hard and lonely life on the prairies," one Pioneer Daughter wrote.

My grandmother was fortunate. She kept her sanity. But somedays the pain would overtake her, and she would take the youngest by the hand and walk off into the field. One of the older boys would go on horseback and get her and bring her back home. As I go through the stories of pioneer women in Dakota, I find many others who also headed across the prairie.

All of my grandmother's fourteen children were born at home, usually with the help of a midwife; only the last one, when complications developed, with the help of a physician.

"In those days, if anyone was ushered into this world with the aid of a doctor, we always wondered what was wrong with them," my father and his siblings laughed.

We don't believe much in doctors to this day. My grandmother cured ailments with her Doctor Book, "Praktischer Fuhrer zur Gesundheit" (Practitioner's Guide to Health) and her arsenal of Watkins carbosalve, Farney's Albenkrieter and camomile tea. After the family got a phone, the neighbors would ring two long and three shorts at all hours, day or night, when someone was sick, and my grandmother would consult the Doctor Book.

During the flu epidemic after the first world war, my grandfather rode farm to farm, a bag of garlic over his saddle, and distributed it to their neighbors to keep them healthy.

The little sugar they ate outside of cooking, lemon drops brought occasionally by their kind and childless Aunt and Uncle Schumacher, kept the children from developing a taste for more. In the summer they munched on rose hips, picked from the wild roses that dotted the fields, unknowingly absorbing enough vitamin C to stave off most anything. Seldom sick, all nine Roesch children have lived to a ripe old age.

Grandma Roesch cooked. Her life revolved around the preparation of food. In the spring, planting her garden, canning in the summer, feeding the threshing crew of sometimes twenty or more in the early fall.

"In the summertime we ate lamb and chicken," my Aunt Annie writes. "Dad would butcher a lamb and mother would fry down all the meat and place it in a ten gallon crock in the cellar, cover the meat with tallow, taking out as much as she needed for a meal and it kept that way for weeks. Dad made dried beef in a wooden barrel with salt. This kept in the grainery for months."

Grandpa yearly drove a large wagon of wheat twenty-five miles to the flour mill early in the morning and returned with it late at night, ground whole and returned in 100 pound sacks for the winter's baking.

Grandma cooked like she had in the old country. Halupsi, or pigs-in-a-blanket as we called the rice, hamburger, cream and tomato wrapped in a cabbage leaf she made for us. Hot potato salad; borscht, a beet red soup; and kuchen, the bread dough with a fruit and custard filling that some call a cake and others a pie. When the children were sick, she made them wine soup, a carry-over from the vineyards they'd kept in Russia. Kuechla was my favorite. She made them for her children to have a treat after school, or "when the boys came by the summer kitchen with a load of hay," Aunt Marie wrote.

I remember my grandma, and later my mother, faces flushed with leaning over the hot grease, frying one kuechla after another, pulling them from the fat and rolling them in powdered sugar, mock-slapping our hands with the wooden spoon as we tried to grab them, still hot, to eat. "Basoof!" — be careful — Grandma Roesch would warn.

It is my Aunt Annie, the youngest of the Roesch children, who has kept the heritage alive. Selected as the German From Russia representative of a four-state area at the Festival of American Folklife, she once demonstrated German-Russian cooking at the Smithsonian Institution in Washington, D.C.

While Grandma Roesch never used a recipe, according to Aunt Marie, her daughter Annie has put down her ingredients so that they can be passed on. This is Anne Roesch Larson's recipe for Schlitz Kuechla:

    3/4 cup sugar
    1/2 tsp. salt
    3 tsp. baking powder
    1 cup milk or cream
    3 eggs
    5 cups all-purpose flour

Mix and roll out on floured board. Cut into triangles; make three cuts, one in the center and one on each side close, not way out to the edge. Pull the point through the center. Deep fry in hot lard or other shortening, same as doughnuts. Sprinkle with sugar if desired. Makes about two dozen.

My grandmother never wrote down her recipes, nor did she write about their trip to America. My grandfather did, and his description follows:

### ABOUT OUR ARRIVAL HERE IN AMERICA
**Written by my Grandfather Frederich Roesch on April 9, 1929**

We departed from our beloved home in Glueckstahl in Southern Russia on September 26, 1898, on a beautiful Sunday morning after many farewells, sorrow and weeping, following the burial of our beloved Son Friederich who died on September 23 after a thirteen day illness with brain fever. He was four years and sixteen days old, a deeply religious child. With sorrowful hearts we took the first step of our journey after praying for guidance from God, through the land of Bergen to Warsaw, across the border of Bremen, Deutschland.

In all we were seventeen families who traveled to the Ocean and on to the Great Ship Kaiser Frederich, on which we arrived safely on the eighth day in the New York harbor. For health reasons, we and others had to remain for eight days in a Hospital Center. Upon our release we continued cross country by train and arrived on October 26, 1898 at Hillsview, South Dakota and were graciously received by Brother-in-law, Henry Gross, who had been anxiously awaiting our arrival, and gladly kept us and remain until we had a farm of our own. We remained until January 17, 1899, when we moved to a farm seven miles East of Eureka owned by Christian Freshla.

There we engaged in buying cattle in partnership with Brother-in-law Jacob Schumacher.

On April 22, 1899 we moved to our present home five miles north of Roscoe, where we enjoyed much good fortune, along with some bad fortune.

We praise the Good Lord, and are ever grateful for the bountiful blessings we have received to this present time. AMEN.

## Susana Weidner Schamber
## Yankton County
## 1875

Susana was born in 1856 at Krohnenthal, Crimea, South Russia, of German parentage. Catherine II the Great, Empress of Russia, seeing the need of land reform and success in raising food, had made a trip through western Europe and found the German farmers most capable, so she invited them to Russia where they would receive certain privileges for producing food. One of these privileges was immunity from conscription for 100 years.

From 1762 until the early 1800's many Germans did accept that promise, immigrated, settling in the Ukraine and the peninsula of Crimea in the Black Sea. Their journeys from their home villages in Germany to Russia were an arduous task. A cart carrying a few personal belongings and household goods, and the younger children, was drawn by an ox, or perhaps a horse. A cow was tied to the cart to provide milk for the children. The adults of the families walked. They traveled in groups, and camped out at night.

But these immigrants became very successful land users, raising small grains and fruits. Since most of these were of the Lutheran faith they built their own schools for their children.

As was the custom, children of the poorer families often were hired out to other farmers. So it was that Susana worked for one Peter Schamber of Friedenthal, Crimea, not far from her birthplace, from childhood through her teens. During the drought and grasshopper days of our "dirty thirties" she well recalled and described how in her childhood the farmers of Crimea had been plagued by grasshoppers in such great numbers that the trees even were stripped bare and completely covered by the hordes of voracious insects.

Back in the late 1700's one Ludweg Chambre, French army officer in Alsace-Lorraine, wanted to migrate to Russia. But he was not eligible. He left his service to France, moved into nearby Switzerland, forsook his Catholic faith for

Lutheran and changed his name to the German-sounding Schamber. Now going into Germany he could migrate to Crimea as a German farmer, which he did in 1803. He possibly accompanied Duc de Richelieu. He settled in Friedenthal and married. Two sons and three daughters were born. In 1874, the younger son, Martin, accompanied by his nephew, John, both educated as teachers, emigrated to the U.S.A. to seek their fortune.

At the age of eighteen, Susana Weidner was married to Peter II, John's elder brother. Their older sister, Rosina, was married to Joseph Bohrer on the same day. In the meantime, Martin Schamber had written from America for them all to come here; there was free land to be had for the asking out of Yankton, Dakota Territory.

On May 26, 1875, the elder Peter Schambers emigrated from Crimea, taking with them their entire family of six children. John was already here. Peter II, wife Susana, Rosina and husband, Joseph Bohrer, were included. A sister of Peter I, Margaret, either came with them or came later. The Schambers had received emigration permission from the German government at the time of emigration to Russia, according to petitions checked in Stuttgart. Thus Martin Schamber was instrumental in bringing his relatives, including Susana, to the United States.

Martin met the travelers at the Yankton community railroad station, Dakota Territory, on July 16, 1875. It is not quite clear whether the newcomers lived in railroad barracks in Yankton until each family had obtained its own homestead, or if Martin had living quarters for all the family. The railroads often advertised abroad for immigrants and had someone meet them at the point of debarkation to direct them to their destination. At Yankton, the Milwaukee railroad had built barracks for the newcomers that could be used for housing until each family was settled.

Peter and Susana took a homestead six miles south and one mile east of Menu, Yankton County. The counties had been surveyed and created about 1862, at the time of the Homestead Act, passed by Congress. Peter and Susana built their sod home in a low place beside a creek that emptied into the James River and moved in that fall. It was a rolling piece of land, foothills of the James.

Usually the homes and other buildings were erected by "bees," relatives and neighbors all helping. Peter and Susana were true pioneers with the minimum of cash, but each with two bare hands, very capable. The next February their first child was born, Wilhelmina. All things were on a "do it yourself" basis. So Susana cared for the children, cooked (mostly from the foods the farm produced), sewed by hand, cleaned, gardened, helped with whatever field work possible. Peter became interested in horticulture through D. B. Gurney, the seedman, of Yankton. He planted an apple orchard that in time supplied apples for his family, relatives, and friends. He built sod barns for cows, sheep, and horses.

In one instance when Susana was milking a cow, an unpredictable ram rammed into her from behind, spilling her and the milk. Besides other bruises, her collar bone was cracked or broken. There were no doctors or bone specialists available so she received no help for her injuries. The break healed in time but left her somewhat stooped and crippled. The grandchildren knew her as the little crippled grandmother.

She had a quiet, uncomplaining disposition, stout heartedly carrying on her duties as wife and mother, rearing the children in the faith of her fathers.

As soon as Peter could see his way clear he built a very comfortable frame home. That home is still being used by the present owners of the farm.

Since there were no public schools as yet, the children attended the Lutheran Day School of Freeman, often staying with relatives. The Milwaukee railroad had reached Freeman by 1879; the Day School was built in the 1880's. Six daughters and one son blessed the home and received their schooling in the Lutheran School. Often the older ones had to miss school because of work that had to be done. Weekends hummed with activities as each child had his own chores to do, and no school. All were baptized and confirmed in the Lutheran faith. One daughter, Helena, died at the age of eighteen, much to the sorrow of the family, especially the brother, George, who was next older and closer to his sister.

The Schambers lived on the hilly farm from 1875 until 1907. Peter had bought a home in Menu, and now moved his much smaller family there. Susana was busy with her home, the garden, sewing, quilting, her grandchildren, and churchwork, in spite of her old handicap.

Then Peter made a trip to the Bitterroot Valley in western Montana, where he bought some land that was to be irrigated. Being a strong, healthy, restless soul, at the age of sixty-one he sold the Menu home and moved with Susana and Pauline, to Stevensville, Montana. There he raised oats, alfalfa, other small grains, plus apples and cherries from his orchard, all under irrigation, from 1912 until 1929.

Thus were spent the lives of two gallant, hardworking, indomitable pioneers! Their values and labors live on in the lives of their posterity.

# Dorothea Bietz
# Hutchinson and Douglas Counties
# 1879

I, Dorothea Baltzer was born April 19, 1865, at Platz, Besserabia, South Russia. It was in the year 1879 when my parents with their family came to the United States. I was fourteen years old at that time. One of my brothers had come to the United States one year earlier and homesteaded a place near Kaylor, South Dakota, in Hutchinson County. The folks moved in with him and then started building their new home.

The nearest town at that time was Scotland, in Bon Homme County. It consisted of a few business places, such as a store, lumber yard, elevator and a bank.

People did not go to town as often as they go now. The reason for this was that they had to go with horses, and people did not know of buying everything like they do now-a-days. My mother went to town once a year. She saw to it that she got enough material for shirts for the boys and dresses for the girls to last them the whole year, and the same with sugar, rice, flour, prunes, etc.

In the year 1884 I was grown up and met Joseph Bietz. We were married in the fall of the same year. Joe had homesteaded a quarter of prairie in Douglas County the year before. John Litz was his first hired man and went along with Joe to break up prairie and put out watermelon seeds. They raised a large quantity. Joe had a one-room house built of sod. The roof was made of a few planks covered with tall lake grass.

In the spring of 1885 we moved into our little home and started building a new house soon. It was larger than the first one. It was also built of sod, and the barn was built onto the house. This roof was made of roofing lumber like we have at the present time. Laying the sod was very hard work. Joe and I did most of that alone. In September we moved into our new house.

We had to break a few acres of prairie each year with the oxen. It was not as fast as now-a-days. We also had two horses, but had to save them for going places, like we do our cars now-a-days.

Scotland was still the nearest railroad station. When fall came and we were done threshing, the grain, mostly wheat, had to be hauled away. For fear of overworking the horses, we used the oxen again. It took three days to make one trip. The roads at that time angled across the prairie to Scotland.

There was a little village about four miles north of Armour called Grandview but there was no railroad going through, so we could not sell our grain there.

In a few years we had quite a few cows to milk, but of course, no separator. But during that time they built railroads through here. Soon the towns sprang up, towns of Armour, Delmont, Tripp and Parkston. Armour had a little creamery, or what you would call one anyway. They came and got our milk every morning, separated it and then brought the skimmed milk back in the afternoon. In the summer time this was not so good. The poor calves had to drink the thick sour milk. We did not have extra milk coolers like they have now, but we found a way to cool it. The evening milk was poured into ten-gallon cans, then hung down in the well overnight for cooling.

It didn't take too long and Delmont had a little creamery like that, too. Then Joe took the milk to Delmont every day and could come back right away with the skimmed milk. This was a whole lot better already. I guess the calves liked it better too.

Perhaps it would be interesting to mention our first post office, which was about five miles north of Delmont, and it was called Schotzville. The postmistress was Susan Marsh. This was all before Delmont existed.

After all this, things were going pretty good. We didn't work with the oxen any more. Horses were used instead. Of course we experienced several droughts the first years we were out here, and also those terrible blizzards.

Thanks to God, I lived through all this. May the good Lord bless the United States in the future.

# Elizabeth Bauder Max
## Bon Homme County
## 1873

Elizabeth, daughter of John and Frederika Bauder, was born in the village of Groszliebenthal in the province of Bessarabia, South Russia in September, 1855.

She came to America at the age of seventeen with other members of her family. Each one carried a bundle of personal belongings on their backs when they left Russia.

It took them two weeks to come across the Atlantic Ocean. They landed in America the latter part of July, 1873. They came to Yankton County in August of the same year. Then later they made their home on a farm in Bon Homme County.

She, being the oldest one in the family, had to help her father get the wood for fuel from the Missouri River, which was about twenty miles from home. They had to leave early in the morning, drive a team of oxen to the river, saw down the trees, load them on the wagons, and start for home again. It was always dark before they got home and they had to walk most of the way, alongside of the oxen. Their lunch was frozen by the time they got to the river, but they had to eat it that way.

The winters were terribly cold! They never had any overshoes to wear. (She never had any overshoes or rubbers on in all her ninety-four years.) Her coat was just a short one. Her parents never took her along to town to buy her shoes. They would purchase shoes large enough so they could be worn for several years, so she had to wear them that way.

Their meals, with the exception of breakfast, consisted mostly of boiled potatoes, dark bread and no butter. Their daily breakfast was coffee or boiled milk and dark bread with no butter — sometimes they had a small amount of jelly to put on the last slice of bread that they ate.

She was married to Jacob Max in 1875. They built a mud house and barn six miles south of Scotland, still in

Bon Homme County. She helped plow sod with oxen and a walking plow. They were able to buy horses later on to help with the farming and they also put up buildings of wood on their place.

One early morning in 1888, her husband left home to go to Scotland. The sun was shining brightly then; but he got into the worst blizzard they had ever seen, when he was about one mile from town. He thought he was lost since he couldn't see where to go, but the horses kept right on walking. All at once they stopped and was he ever surprised to find he was in town, in front of a building or store where they usually stopped. He had to stay in town for three days, and she didn't know whether he was all right or not, since there were no means of communication in those days.

The dust-storms came later and they were so bad at times that kerosene lamps had to be burned in the daytime. They lasted almost all year round, as there was very little rain in summer and very little snow in winter. They were completely dried out for two years.

Next came the grasshoppers and they took everything, all they left was the corn stalks. They were so thick on the fences that the barbed-wire looked like rope. They were so thick on the fence posts that you couldn't even see the posts.

Mrs. Max made her home with her youngest daughter for the last twenty-one years of her life. She was always able to be up and around, and to go upstairs to her room. She missed only one meal at the table in all that time.

## Eva Kliewer Tieszen
## Turner County
## 1874

Eva was born in 1860 in the Ukraine. She came with her parents to Dakota Territory arriving at Yankton September 5, 1874, and moving a few weeks later to Turner county where her parents homesteaded in the area near where Marion is located. The Kliewer family was part of the settlement of Mennonites who came to Dakota territory in 1874. The Kliewers were originally from Friesland in the Netherlands, had emigrated to the Germanies, and from there to the Ukraine.

On February 13, 1879 she was married to Peter P. Tieszen who had also been born in the Ukraine, in 1849, and who had come to Dakota Territory in 1874 as part of the same movement of Mennonites. He was homesteading a farmstead two miles west of where Marion is located. He had been previously married; his first wife died.

Life on the prairies was hard. Their first home could be described as no more than a shack. They plowed with oxen at first, and several years after their marriage, when they obtained their first team of horses, family legend says the couple cried for joy. When they had only oxen, even a trip to see her parents nine miles away, was a major undertaking.

She became the mother of a large family. Her children who lived were eight; several children also died in infancy. She and her husband lived their entire lives on the farm which they had homesteaded.

Her education was limited to the short and infrequent common schools available during her childhood. She was a lifelong member of the Bethesda Mennonite Church.

Years after her death, her children remembered her as a family peacemaker, an even tempered woman who disliked controversy and worked hard to harmonize differences. She loved flowers and brightened her homestead with flowers from her flower garden. Her husband had developed a good sized orchard, partly as a hobby and partly to augment food supplies. This was probably one of the better orchards in early Turner county.

submitted by D.W. Tieszen

## Huether Bitz Orth
## McPherson County
## Before 1889

She and her husband and approximately six of their children came over from Russia, filed for a homestead, and began very frugally to farm. This was on what was to be the future site of Eureka.

There were rumors that a railroad was to be built to this site, which soon became a reality. Work was begun on laying the tracks and since she was the only woman in the area she soon found herself cooking meals for the crew. The children gathered buffalo chips and anything else that could be used as fuel for cooking. The well-deserved rest she needed by night was also sacrificially given so that she might bake large amounts of bread which was quickly consumed again the next day making it necessary to bake a like amount every night.

As the train became operational many new settlers arrived and the city of Eureka began to grow.

True to their religious principles, they felt the need of a place of worship. Each family was assigned a certain number of "Batza" or sun-dried clay bricks which were carefully turned and dried in the sun. On a set day, the "Batza" were loaded on stone-boats or "rutches" and drawn by oxen to the site they had selected and everyone helped to erect the first church.

Having lost their homestead and with no reimbursement, they moved on again in a true pioneering spirit to find land and make a home where they could farm.

This took them through North Dakota and on into Canada following the course of the Red River which, when necessary, provided fish for food. They constructed a small canoe-type boat for better fishing. One day she found that the older boys had left the boat untied and it was drifting down the river with her youngest child aboard. They had neglected to help her out of the boat. She had some very grave experiences until the boat was recovered.

They had lived for a while close to a Colony of Mennonites in Canada who were very kind to them and provided a midwife who helped out in a difficult delivery.

Her husband contracted tuberculosis and was very ill. One winter day they were in need of several essential items as well as medicine for her husband that would require a trip to town. This would have to be made on foot. Not having any shoes she wore those of her husband. Leaving very early in the morning she made the request that they keep a light in the window at night so that she might find her way home. She walked to town, got the supplies and on her way home after dark lost her way. She saw lights and tried to follow them finding that they were only the glaring eyes of timber-wolves surrounding her. Through faith and prayer she did return home late but safely.

Her husband died in Canada and she again returned to Eureka with five of her youngest children, the four older ones having married and settled down in Canada. She returned mainly because of her loneliness and because her husband's brother, Daniel Bitz, lived in Eureka with his family and had a small grocery store there.

In approximately 1915 she married my father Peter Orth of Mound City who had been widowed two years earlier and had some motherless children who needed care.

I was not aware of it at the time but feel very deeply now of the sacrifice she again made to take on another family to raise after bringing up nine of her own. She taught us to cook, mend and clean, making the best of whatever we had and learning to do without the things we didn't have.

Besides that, she taught us the sometimes harder lessons of obedience, promptness, truthfulness, respect and all the other things essential to becoming what any mother has a right to expect us to become.

by Ella Orth (Mrs. Konrad) Deibert

# THE GERMANS

## Emily Hoffmann Baumgarten
## Edmunds County
## 1885

Emily was born in Oschatz, Germany, in 1862. The older brother and sisters gradually migrated to America and after the father's death, Emily and her mother joined them when Emily was fifteen years old.

Thus started a long life in a new country. Emily and her mother made the voyage alone. Her mother was ill most of the way, but comforted Emily with her cheerfulness and courage. Emily related an incident which occurred on the voyage. Her mother asked for some hot tea and Emily went in search of someone to help her. As she wandered about, a large wave washed in through a port hole. She felt herself carried along by the force of the water. Suddenly she was rescued by a white-faced sailor, who begged her for a promise not to tell what had happened, for it had been his responsibility to keep the port hole closed. A very wet and bedraggled young woman went back to her mother.

Emily's brother Carl had written to a friendly minister who met the two in New York City and placed them safely on a train, westward bound for Tomah, Wisconsin.

Eight years later, at Tomah, Emily Hoffmann and George Louis Baumgarten were united in marriage. After their marriage in 1885, Mr. Baumgarten left immediately for the Dakota territory where he had previously filed on a claim near Kelly, a town no longer in existence. The termination of the railroad was at Ipswich, about thirty-five miles away. After Mr. Baumgarten had erected a home for his bride, she joined her husband to enter a life far different from that she had ever known.

Always having lived within a close community, Emily Baumgarten suddenly found herself transplanted into a strange environment. Far as the eye could see stretched a vast grassy plain, the only sign of life, a hawk swooping down over the horizon, or the swish of a prairie animal scuttling away through the grass. At night across the lonely plain came the fearful and startling wail of the coyote, an awesome sound for ears unschooled in the ways of the prairie. Small wonder that the bride passed through a period of homesickness and longing for the home and friends she had left in Wisconsin. When the cabin became unbearably lonely, Emily would join her husband in the fields and follow along the freshly upturned sod, mile after mile.

But in time the nostalgia passed and Mrs. Baumgarten set about becoming a true pioneer wife, which meant forgetting self in meeting the demands involved in everyday living. Here and there cabins came to dot the landscape as other young couples came to start the great adventure of building homes in a new country.

Compared with modern methods and conveniences the life of the pioneer must seem crude indeed. No man was sufficient unto himself, but each must needs on the helpfulness of his neighbor. Out of this need grew deep and lasting friendships. Harvest time, threshing time, well digging, found all working together.

Emily Baumgarten gave freely of her services at the bedside of the ill and afflicted. Sometimes aroused at night by the frantic knocking on the door, she would hurriedly answer the call. The two would make their way back through the darkness where Emily would minister at a neighbor's bedside. There was no time now to pine for the home in Wisconsin. All her efforts must needs be focused on the problem at hand, and only after she had done all possible, would she return to the duties awaiting in her home. In giving service to others the years passed quickly indeed.

What had at first consisted of a vast grassy plain had now changed into a friendly community. In every direction new homes had come into being. As the community grew, the need of a school was felt and in time the little white school house over the hill became a reality.

Here it was that two little girls from the Baumgarten home began their education on that important first day of school! The schoolhouse was also the center of community interest. The spiritual and cultural needs of the people were met through church and literary societies. Everyone took an active part in entertaining, which is a richer experience than being a mere listener.

The railroad terminal was now at Bowdle, six miles away.

No pioneer story would be complete without an account of crop failures, prairie fires, blizzards and an Indian scare, with perhaps a cyclone thrown in for good measure, all of which came within the experience of Emily Baumgarten. During those first tearful months in her new home, Emily was cheered by the thought that after a year or two they would return to Wisconsin. Crops were good that first year, as they were the second and third year, until finally there was no thought of leaving their firmly established home. Then followed years of drought and privation. Once a cyclone tore through the prairie two miles to the north, destroying the lives and home of an elderly couple, while Emily and her husband sadly viewed the tragedy.

Prairie fires followed in quick succession. Early one April such a fire swooped out of the west, totally destroying the Baumgarten barn with livestock involved. All of the frantic fighting with gunny sacks and pails of water was of no avail. With weary bodies and blackened faces neighbors stood helplessly by, watching the fire take its toll.

Mrs. Baumgarten had another experience with fire, but with a happier ending. She was baking bread when the stove pipe caught fire and in turn, the roof. Having only her own resourcefulness to turn to, she dragged a ladder to the scene and quickly extinguished the blaze, as well as the fire in the stove. But the bread remained to be baked. Packing it firmly in the box of a small hand sled, Emily made her way across the prairie to the home of a good neighbor, where she finished baking the bread.

In direct contrast to the dreaded prairie fires was the equally dreaded blizzard. Today it may be a terrible experience to be lost in a blizzard, but at that time there were few landmarks or fences to guide one's way. So intense and severe were the storms that Emily would beg her husband to tie a clothesline around his waist while going to the barn to do chores. The other end she fastened securely to the door knob. Emily was taking no chances in allowing her husband to become involved in the fearful and icy grip of a prairie blizzard.

Along with the natural hazards and problems of pioneer life came the Indian scare of 1890. This story has often been related by the parents within the family group. On this particular day, Mr. and Mrs. Baumgarten awakened to a day clear and serene. Too serene! The highway passed close by and was usually the scene of busy country traffic. But not a vehicle passed by. Off to the fields no one was going to work. As they scanned the landscape on all sides, no sign of human life could be seen. Puzzled, they consulted the almanac. Might they have made a mistake in dates and perhaps this was Sunday?

The day wore on and Mrs. Baumgarten busied herself making a shirt. During the late afternoon a neighbor drove into the yard. Why had they not gone to Bowdle, were they not afraid of the Indians? Indians? What Indians? It seems that in the general confusion no one had warned them and what had been a frightening experience to the neighbors had been a peaceful and untroubled night to them. However, Mrs. Baumgarten, with two small girls clinging to her skirts, went in search of her husband and begged him to leave for Bowdle at once. It was near evening and Mr. Baumgarten argued that if the Indians were really on the war path, they would burn everything that lay before them and a glowing horizon would give warning of their approach. Somewhat doubtfully Emily went back to the house to finish the shirt and have it ready just in case! But nothing happened and before long people were returning to their homes and tranquility was restored, not to be disturbed again by Indians.

However, pioneer life had its lighter moments. The thrifty and ever resourceful pioneer had learned methods of combining business with pleasure. Wild fruits grew in abundance along the beautiful Missouri river and gathering the fruit furnished an opportunity for a pleasant outing. Mrs. Baumgarten, with her family and friends, would pack lunch and bedding in a lumber wagon or democratic wagon and away they would go for a short camping trip along the river.

They would return laden with different varieties of wild fruits which made delicious preserves and jellies, a welcome addition to the diet of a prairie pioneer.

The Fourth of July celebrations were truly colorful events and Bowdle was the scene of these celebrations. The women came forth in elaborate costumes of silks and satins, picture hats and lacy parasols. Entertainment varied, but there must always be a ball game, a band concert, a bowery dance and a patriotic speech. The bowery was built of fragrant new lumber and fresh green boughs brought miraculously from somewhere. To such a celebration came Mrs. Baumgarten and her family. All had been up since early dawn in busy preparation, the little girls anxiously scanning the sky and now dressed in stiffly starched white dresses, while Mother packed the inevitable lunch. As the years passed, neighbors would gather once a year in some shady grove to partake in friendly communion and thus The Old Settlers Picnic came into being. Here it was that the pioneers paused in their daily tasks to enjoy a bit of fellowship and recreation.

Mrs. Baumgarten often expressed her joy and delight when she set foot in America. She has given a lifetime of love and loyalty to her adopted country.

## Amalia Oppenheimer Colman
## Lawrence County
## 1877

Amalia was born in 1852 in the small town of Schluchtern, near Frankfort on the Main, Germany. Her Father, Michel Oppenheimer, was a writer and translator of Hebrew and Jewish religious works. The first seventeen years of her life were spent in Schluchtern.

Following the death of her Mother, she came to the United States to visit relatives in Baltimore, Maryland. After a short stay in Baltimore, she made the long trip across the United States to Denver, Colorado, where she had relatives. In Denver, she met Nathan Colman, also a German-Jewish immigrant, and they were married in 1874.

When the gold rush to the Black Hills began in 1876, Mr. Colman decided to join the many settlers in the new Territory of Dakota, and in February, 1877, he arrived in Deadwood, where he was to spend the remaining years of his life. By April of the same year, Mr. Colman had prepared a home for his family who had remained in Denver, and early in that month, Mrs. Colman and small daughter made the long, hazardous trip by stage coach to join her husband in Deadwood. The stage coach trip was made by way of Sidney, Nebraska. Bands of marauding Indians frequently attacked the stage coaches in those early days. On the day of Mrs. Colman's arrival in Deadwood, a delay in schedule gave rise to the rumor that the stage had been attacked, so many anxious moments were spent by Mr. Colman and others who awaited its arrival.

The life of the pioneer family was a difficult one, and many hardships beset Mr. and Mrs. Colman during these early days in Deadwood. Two sons and four daughters were born to them here, of whom only three daughters survived. Two sons and two daughters died in diphtheria epidemics and of other early day diseases which were difficult to control in those days.

In September of the year 1879, when the town of Deadwood was almost totally destroyed by fire, Mrs. Colman and a little son who was only a few days old, had to be removed from their home, which was in the path of the fire. Home and business were wiped out in this fire, and once again, in 1894, the family was to lose both home and business in a destructive fire.

Mr. Colman, a naturalized citizen of the United States, took an active part in the growth of the community. In 1878 he was appointed Postmaster for a small precinct known as Beaver, adjacent to Deadwood. He acted as one of the Judges of the Territorial Election held in the year 1889, when South Dakota became a State, and was several times a Delegate to State Republican Conventions thereafter. For many years he was a Justice of the Peace in Deadwood. He was the leader of the Jewish community in religious observances until the time of his death in 1906.

Mrs. Colman continued to make her home in Deadwood until her death in 1939.

Charlotte Catharina Reitman Bottcher

## Charlotte Catharina Reitman Bottcher
## Hyde County
## 1883

Charlotte was born in Hanover, Germany in 1850. She spent the first fourteen years of her life at home with her parents and attended school in Hanover, but at that early age she began to work in the homes of others for she was well-schooled in the art of housekeeping and homemaking. In Hanover she met William Bottcher who had been sent there and apprenticed to a carpenter and cabinet maker that he might learn that trade, and he learned it well. After completing his apprenticeship, he, with three brothers, came to the United States and settled in New York state in the town of Elmira. The Pullman Car Company was then making their sleepers to be used on the trains and he at once found work at finishing the interior of these cars.

In due time William sent for Charlotte to come to Elmira to marry him. This she was willing to do and they were married in Elmira, New York in 1866 and established their home there. There they became the parents of three sons.

In 1883 the cry of "Free Land" was heard ringing around the world and they decided that they, too, with their family should take advantage of this offer of land to be had just for making some improvements and living on it. This sounded to them, and to countless others, like a marvelous offer. They knew this Dakota was a new land and to make a home there would require plenty of hard work but hard work seems to have been one thing that they were not afraid of.

So in 1883, shortly after their baby girl Emma was born, Mr. Bottcher and his sons started out for Dakota in an emigrant car to make a new home in the west. He filed on land, built a sod house and sent for his wife to come and she came bringing Emma, a six month old baby, in her arms. The sod house did have a plank floor which was almost a luxury in those early days; many a homesteader had just the dirt floor. The sod house was heated with a straw burner stove and there the family lived for ten years during which time two more sons were born.

A half-sister of Mrs. Bottcher came to Dakota also and they filed on land in Spink County; however, they, like many other homesteaders didn't stay long, but returned to the east. In later years this half-sister came out and made her home with the Bottchers and died there.

Mr. Bottcher was blessed with the "know how" to do things in building, repairing machinery and in almost everything that was necessary to the homesteaders in this land which was so newly settled. It is interesting to note that of his six sons, it was Ed who seemed to inherit that ability to fix anything that needed fixing. The Bottcher's neighbors and some not near enough to be called neighbors, soon learned that Will Bottcher seemed to be able to fix or do almost anything that required doing and would call on him for help in an emergency. He was never known to be too busy to help someone out who desperately needed his help. This Will Bottcher was not idle in winter; he used any spare time he might have in repairing the harness for the oxen which were the only animals they had for work or transportation in those days.

The time came when Will could buy the horses which they had need for and longed to have. It was toward evening when he arrived home with the new team. Can you not imagine the whole family gathering around admiring those beautiful animals? But they must get at the evening chores so they went about their work and then darkness came and they were afraid to unharness the team for the night ,for how were they to know which buckles to unfasten? Mr. Bottcher, having been a city man, was no wiser in this than his sons. After a family conference they decided they had better leave the harness on all night, then take it off by daylight so they could study the problem and, of course, solve it. This was always a family joke and they could always laugh about the quandary they were in that night.

They had to haul water for three miles for all household use and that was such an inconvenience that the Bottchers decided to dig a well where they thought water might be found. They went to work at that and got water just as they had thought they would and with keeping the well cleaned and in good repair, that well served the Bottchers as long as they owned the farm.

Then came the big new house which Mr. Bottcher built up on the hill near the well. He bought a new hard coal heater which was pure luxury and their home became a gathering place for people near and far. Here were held many neighborhood parties, quilting bees, Larkin Club meetings and the many things that this fun-loving family enjoyed so very much. Here another son was born. The entire family loved music and were a musical group. Emma played the organ, the boys played the violin and banjo, and Mr. Bottcher the accordion so they had quite a musical group in their own family. At the parties they would play cards for hours, have lunch, and then dance until morning was about to come.

Mr. Bottcher built a dam, and as far as this writer knows, it was the first dam to be built in Hyde County. Here they skated in winter, swam in summer and the boys even built a boat to be used on the lake formed by the water in the dam.

Church services were held at the Harno home with a minister coming out from Wolsey to conduct services for these pioneer families. The Bottchers were regular attendants at these meetings. Rev. Leyhe was the pastor who ministered to the people in this neighborhood.

In school in Germany, Charlotte had learned to do all kinds of handwork which were not only useful, to say the least, during the days on the farm and when she was raising her family, but in later years she spent many happy hours at her needlework or knitting, the arts she had learned in her youth.

It is interesting to note that the doll she dressed for her little daughter in those long ago years is still dressed in the clothes made then and is now eighty-one years old.

During those early years in Dakota Mrs. Bottcher was, indeed, a very busy woman. She made all the family's clothing, even the men's underwear (often made of flour sacks) and knitted stockings and socks and mittens for the family. It was she who made all the clothing for the men as well as dresses for herself and Emma until Emma learned to sew.

The family slept, for many years, on straw ticks, often filled with corn husks. The grain sacks had to be mended to make them last as long as possible.

Threshing time was a very busy time for all the homesteaders. The threshing was done by horse power, which required sixteen men and eight horses. Sixteen men to cook for was a big job but Mrs. Bottcher was equal to all the planning for the meals and the work of cooking them. One can well imagine that threshing time at the Bottchers was not only a busy but happy time for there the neighbors gathered to help so that they, in turn, might have the help of the Bottchers. Mrs. Bottcher and her daughter often went in to help the neighbor women with the work of cooking for the threshing crew.

During the years when there was a wheat crop Mr. Bottcher would take a load of wheat to Miller, where there was a mill, and bring home a load of flour. This huge amount of flour would be used up in the good bread which Mrs. Bottcher baked twice each week and two ovensful at each baking, not to mention the other baked goods which appeared on the Bottcher's table.

Black birds were so numerous some years that the children were sent out to the fields with tin pans to pound and scare the birds away from the precious crops.

There was wild fruit to be preserved and canned for the winter and each Christmas time an Uncle Henry in New York would send out nuts and tobacco.

Mrs. Bottcher made trips back to the old home in Elmira and would fill the bottom of her trunk with apples to bring back to Dakota to the family.

The school teacher was often boarded by the Bottchers so that their children might have the advantage of going to school. When Uncle Henry sent apples out for Christmas the children had an apple in their lunch bucket which, in those days, was a real treat often to be shared with their school friends.

Later when Emma grew up, she, too, taught school. She would often plan basket socials and entertainments to earn money for the school so that they might have an organ in the school house. This was not only for school use since those little school houses became the gathering place for the community. There the literary society met and there were spell downs, another of the entertainments for the pioneers, and to have an organ was the ambition of every school. Once a basket at Emma's social sold for $5.00, an unheard-of price to pay for a basket, but the man who bought that basket had heard that that particular basket contained cream puffs. Could it be, do you think, that that basket was Emma's and that one of her six brothers could have let that secret out of the bag?

The Bottchers always had their own meat. The men took care of the butchering but to care for all that meat meant a lot of work for the womenfolk of the family. The homemade sausage was so good and a much better table could be set for them. That work was willingly and cheerfully done. Then she made root beer, maintained a large garden (which could be irrigated from the well), surplus vegetables were canned for winter's use, and some could be, and were, dried.

Back of the barn stood the chicken house, which was Mrs. Bottcher's special project. There she raised chickens for their use but also to sell, many dozens of eggs sold for not more than eight cents a dozen. Not only did she make all the butter the family could use, but each week she had twenty-five to forty pounds packed in a tub, for the shipping day in the little village of Highmore was on Tuesday. For that good butter she would receive sixteen cents a pound.

Money had a different value in those days. Emma's salary at school where she often taught all eight grades was never more than twenty-five to thirty dollars a month.

Mr. Bottcher died in 1904 and Mrs. Bottcher stayed on the farm and with the help of her sons, then still at home, continued to operate it. Finally, with more of the sons striking out for themselves, she sold out and bought a home near to her daughter's home in Highmore.

## Wilhemeina Klipstine Yada Haack
## Codington County
## 1879

Mrs. Wilhemeina Yada Haack, nee Klipstine, was born in Prussia, Germany in 1846. She came to America by sail boat in 1861, and was married to Charles Yada in Dodge County, Wisconsin in 1867. They farmed at Denzer, Wisconsin until coming to the Dakota Territory, Codington County in the Spring of 1879. However their lucky number for a homestead and tree claim led them to North Hand County. Mr. Yada filed on the above mentioned land in Park Township in 1882.

In the Spring of 1883 he moved his family and their equipment to their new home. They made the trip to Redfield, South Dakota by railroad, then overland by team and wagon to their homestead twenty-five miles west of Redfield. Mr. Yada had built a small claim shanty before bringing his family to Hand County. There were now seven children.

Floor space was at a premium, because the shack measured a little over twelve feet square. They had to store the seed wheat for the next crop in a good place, so it also was stored in the shack. The beds were made on the wheat bin.

Neighbors came in to help the Yadas get things in readiness for living. A well had to be put down by pick and shovel in those days. When at the depth of five or six feet they were surprised to find a glittering, flaky, bright coppery substance which resembled ground-up copper. This vein was about the size of a man's arm. Excitement ran high. A good specimen was carefully stored, after all agreed that it should be assayed. However, mails and transportation were most undependable, consequently there was little time for chasing such bubbles, since the goal of every man was to wrest from this new soil, the food that was needed to sustain life in these new surroundings. In the rush to make a living, it is understandable that the prized package was lost and finally all but forgotten, as a Will-O'-The-Wisp.

Had time and circumstances permitted a proper follow-up of this incident, much of interest might have been revealed.

It is inspiring to know at this time, how much time and energy were willingly expended to make available all that was needed by the newcomers to their new home. Everyone put their best foot forward to be a good neighbor.

About three miles distant, another family, Sawyer by name, was holding down their claim or homestead. A roomy sod house was their abode. In a small lean-to a blacksmith shop was operated by the father. This was a great help to the new settlers. His wife ran a small store in their home, with just the most necessary things for the house and land. This little store was supplied biweekly by a wagon trip to Redfield about twenty-eight miles distant. On these trips the accumulated mail was also brought to the little community's U.S. Post Office, which was in a corner of the sod house.

Much time and energy were cheerfully rendered by all these new settlers in the endeavor to be a good and helpful neighbor.

Crops of wheat, corn, oats, potatoes, turnips, melons and all garden vegetables were planted and satisfying crops were reaped.

After the spring's work, a frame house was erected on the extreme north end of the homestead because this proved to be a better building site. This structure measured about thirty-four feet square, and boasted two rooms upstairs, together with one large room on the first floor. For those days this was considered a rather spacious home.

The family eagerly moved into the new house here on the boundless prairies. They worked hard to establish a real home.

During these early years this home was a favorite gathering place for any and all church denominations. Church services were held for all, as there were no church buildings built at this time. For seats or pews, planks and grocery boxes (these were strong packing cases at this time) were brought in for the friends and neighbors that came to church services.

In 1886 the newly organized Sunday School celebrated Christmas Eve by having a lighted tree and a program in the Yada School house. That was on the Northwest corner of the Yada homestead, about one-fourth of a mile from their home. The weather was beautiful until the close of the program, when a fierce blizzard blew in. What should they do now? Many present had come by lumber wagon drawn by horse or ox team. All were from six to ten miles from home. In all about twenty friends spent the night. Straw-ticks and feather beds were put on the floor with plenty of pillows and blankets and quilts to keep warm and snug. With the base burner giving warmth and light, everyone was soon at rest, safe from the howling blizzard that swept over the open prairies all through the night.

Morning dawned with the storm abated. Everyone enjoyed a hearty breakfast after which all were speeded homeward, though the going was difficult as all the trails were covered with drifted snow. Everyone reached their homes safe and grateful to their friends for a safe night's shelter from the storm.

No Dakota pioneer can forget the awful blizzard of January, 1888. At that time the Yada household stored the fuel (coal and other fuels) in a shed about three rods from the kitchen door; only one large chunk of coal was near the house. The fierce and suddenness of the storm cancelled the chances of getting any more to the house. Mr. Yada rationed that chunk of coal to the big kitchen stove in such a way that it cooked the day's food, and also somewhat warmed the house. The base burner, at other times in use, was not kept going. Because of the storm, the children were not permitted to start for school. They donned all their wraps and went to bed to keep warm and to stay until coal could be brought in at almost noon the next day.

This storm was indeed a most disastrous one, for many lost their bearings because of the blowing snow and were left to the mercy of the elements. Three such cases were known within a few miles of the Yada farm. Their spent bodies were found buried in snowdrifts. Many school children were counted among its victims, as the storm struck just as they were on their way to school. It might be of interest to note that every pioneer home had a cellar underneath the house where all cured meats and vegetables were stored for the winter's use. After this first of many blizzards, many families also stored their fuel in the cellar so it would be handy in case of an emergency.

To be a good Mother and neighbor in those days meant more than being a bridge player or knowing how to apply a perfect face make-up. Much of the farm chores and gardening as well as all household duties were left to the women and children. The men worked in the fields from early to late.

Mother Yada always had a bounteous garden, a large poultry flock, did all the family sewing – even making all the denim overalls and jackets. Besides this, she was a master at the spinning wheel, and made all the wool yarn which she then knitted into stockings and mittens for her family of nine children, herself, and husband.

Neighbors and friends could always depend on her as a nurse and midwife. The nearest doctor was twenty-five miles distant, so she was willing to answer any call for help, night or day. Many a life was ushered into this world by her aid given to the pioneer women of her locality. Truly, she could count "her" babies by the hundred.

Undertakers were unknown in these new areas. When lives were spent, she ministered to the grieving, and prepared for the burial the bodies of many whose spirit had winged its way into the beyond.

In 1889 a drought set in and crops failed. Because a loan could not be paid the family lost the homestead. They moved onto their tree claim to continue farming there. This quarter section was about two miles east of the homestead.

More misfortune followed. Here Mother lost her husband, also her oldest daughter in November of the year 1890. Then her oldest son was killed by a bolt of lightning during a storm in the harvest season of 1891.

Her courage was her best asset. She now filed the tree claim as her homestead. She stuck to the old farm and made good with the children's help, keeping things going until 1894 when she married Carl Haack. They continued to make this farm their home. In 1898 the final proof was made for her homestead. Much satisfaction was derived from the fact that she was able in 1904 to erect a new house on her farm and a new barn in 1906.

Then in 1908 she and her husband rented their farm and retired to a new cottage in Rockham, South Dakota,

Faulk County. There they lived in peace and contentment until the fall of 1924, when she fell and broke her hip, passing away at the Faulkton Hospital October 5, 1924. She was laid to rest in the cemetery at Rockham where so many of her friends had preceded her.

    She will always be remembered as a devout Christian whose courage and faith in God's promise is an inspiration to all who knew her.

This was written by her youngest daughter, Mrs. R.A. Mielke (Amanda). Mother was known as Grandma Haack to all the children of Rockham and country around.

## Rosina Schoessler
## Davison County
## 1882

She was eight when they left their small Prussian village near Breslau to come to America. There, they had been told, was a land of great opportunity and freedom. Enroute through Bremen, they saw their first oranges. Her mother, not knowing much about them, bought one. The fragrance was beautiful. The family passed it around, enjoying the perfume of the fruit until it finally was so far gone that it was tossed overboard at sea. That was 1882.

After three stormy weeks at sea—New York. Finally, after more problems, many of them due to their inability to understand the language, they arrived on their homestead, twenty-five miles southeast of Mt. Vernon.

It took three days to make the trip to Mitchell and back. This was by ox-team. One day going, one day to rest the animals and do the trading, and one day home. Mitchell was then a sprawling, dirty, shanty town.

A sod house was built. Fields were plowed and life had begun in America. There was drought; the wheat was insufficient for their own needs. A rat plague followed during which possessions were dragged from their sod house and ruined. Clothing was put into the oven at night to save it from the rats. But the will to survive was strong and the people withstood the pressures.

She worked in the fields and followed a walking plow for miles. In fact, in her garden at Reliance, on a platform, stands an old-fashioned walking plow that the junk man was going to break up for junk. When she saw it she asked to buy it. To her, it was part of her life and something worth saving. God Bless the junk man, he gave it to her and set it up in the garden.

She has had the pleasure of seeing the country develop from the ox-team to the speed of jet travel. Lunch in Pierre and dinner in Los Angeles. She made the remark to me one day not too long ago, as we drove along the railroad track, "You know, Rose, I saw the railroad come and I believe I am going to live to see it go."

Originally published in *South Dakota Newsletter,* April, 1964, page 3.

## Anna Katherina Rosenmeier Stuempge
## Turner County
## 1879

Anna Katherina Rosenmeier was born in southwestern Germany near France in 1827. She never knew her mother who died when Katherina was very young. From the time she was eight or nine years old she was living with strangers working for her living. She found life so hard that sometimes when picking up potatoes she would hide some to roast later in the fields. To make her clothes, she beat up flax straw to weave into material.

When she was twenty-eight her great opportunity came. Two of her chums were coming to America with their folks, they had tickets bought when one of the girls suddenly became ill and died. They asked Katherina if she wanted to go to America in the girl's place, using the ticket and working it out. She worked for this family at Sheboygan, Wisconsin until she married Henry Stuempges.

Henry Stuempges was also born in southwestern Germany near the French border in 1826. He came to Sheboygan County, Wisconsin with his parents, brothers, and sister Johanna in 1849. They bought timber land which the government was selling cheap, but they could buy only eighty acres. The government man took them to the land and said, "Here's your land. Here's where you can build your house," so they took their tools and before nightfall had built the walls of their log cabin for protection in the woods. Later, after they had become lumbermen, they built their mother a better home.

The other children had married and Henry was living alone in the log house. He needed a wife, and though he had never met Katherina, he had seen her and admired her in church. Also, he had heard what people were saying, that she had worked long enough to more than pay for her passage to America. Furthermore, she was a good worker, so soon thereafter he went to see her, dressed up and wearing the

Anna Katherina Rosenmeier Stuempge

silk hat he had brought along from Germany where he had been a weaver of silk and also had sold silk clothes and hats.

Katherina looked up from her barnyard chores, thrilled to see such a fine-looking young man standing there; indeed, a storybook Prince Charming. But she was embarrassed in her worst old clothes, and insisted on going to the house to dress up a bit before talking with him. He came right to the point—would she be his wife? They were married in 1856.

Although always a devoted and happy couple, they were very different, having lived in opposite environments. He was truly a gentle, kindhearted man and deeply religious. He had beautiful blue eyes and in later years, snowy white hair. Though of good stature, he was never strong physically, never having done manual labor until he came to Wisconsin. Katherina was darker skinned, with brown eyes, and hardly ever weighing more than one hundred pounds. But she was strong and energetic and always a great help and strength to her husband.

In 1863 Henry moved his wife and four daughters to Clayton County, Iowa, near Monona. There they lived with the Eiferts until they bought a little farm. Etta was six months old and Mina, the eldest, had to watch the younger ones while Henry and Katherina worked in the fields. Wheat sold for $4.00 per bushel and Katherina went into the neighboring fields gathering loose grain that the men did not get into bundles; she would stack it near theirs and later they would thresh it for her.

Then they bought eighty acres of land from Charles Lang six miles east of Monona. A few years later they bought twenty acres of black walnut timber land and eighty acres of fire-swept land which had very few large trees, mostly it was bushes growing among stumps from which new shoots had sprung. During the summer Henry usually had men helping him grub out the stumps. Clearing the timberland for cultivation was hard work and only three to six acres could be cleared in a summer, but the soil was very rich and wheat went thirty bushels to the acre. In the winter the men were busy trimming and cutting up wood to sell. One winter he had them cut about 100 cord in the black walnut timber where the trees were very large. This he sold to be used for railroad ties.

He needed $300.00 to pay the ten percent interest he owed on $3000.00 he had borrowed when he bought the last eighty acres of land. He had borrowed from an unscrupulous man who later foreclosed when hard years came, before Henry had a chance to get matters handled. They always had a difficult time financially and the girls had to help others to get a little spending money. One of their worries came when a carpenter wanted to collect $100.00 about a year after he had been paid. Henry couldn't find the receipt and even the clock refused to run. Katherina took it down for Henry to look over; she noticed a paper and showed it to Henry—so there was the lost paper and all that was wrong with the clock was that it had been forgotten.

In June, 1879, Henry drove a team of three-year old colts to Dakota Territory to homestead in Turner County. When he returned to Iowa he left the colts in August Kuhler's pasture. The Kuhlers were former neighbors in Iowa who had come to Dakota a year earlier and lived eight miles southwest of Henry's claim. In October that year Henry Stuempges had a sale in Iowa. He kept two horses, two small colts, four cows and some chickens. The stock and all of the belongings came to Dakota in one railroad car for $100.00. He and his son Henry came in the same car so they could care for the stock on the way.

Katherina and the other three children took the train which went only so far as Canton. From there they took the freight which went only to Parker, twenty miles north of their destination. They got to Parker about 10 a.m. the second day and loaded their things on the wagon to start south on the prairie road. The colts were tied to the wagon and they drove the cows. The village of Swan Lake, now called Hurley, was about half way and here they stopped at a farm house to spend the night. The friendly Danish family invited them in for a good supper of dark flour biscuits and barley coffee. Beds were made by putting hay on the floor and spreading blankets over.

By noon the next day they had reached their destination. There they lived with a family by the name of Whitmarsh who lived a mile south of where Henry and his son-in-law, Salon Gaylord, were building a house. Salon had married Hanna and they had come to Dakota a year earlier. She was sick all winter with an illness the doctors called "spinal fever" and died in the spring. She was buried in the Yankton cemetery, her grave being the first one. Later, when Etta and Mary were working in Yankton, they walked out several times, but now knowing that some of the graves were marked with numbers, never found which one was Hanna's.

It didn't take long to build their one-story, three-room house. The inside walls were not plastered, just covered with boards. Later, after August married, he built a new house using this old part for the kitchen. When they first came to Dakota they got their mail once a week from a post office in a house near Wakonda about eight miles away; later a neighbor one and one-half miles away had the post office. Centerville was about eight miles but had only one store. So, even though it took them a day, they usually went to Yankton to do their shopping and to market their butter and eggs.

Katherina was a Lutheran, but in Iowa they were members of Henry's church, the German Reformed. After a few years this church was discontinued and they joined a German Methodist church and were Methodists so long as they lived. In Iowa, three Methodist churches under one pastorate had union, or quarterly, meetings every three months. This was a great one-day meeting beginning with services in the forenoon, dinner, and another service at 2:30. All who lived within in two miles of the church took someone home with them for a hurried dinner which had been prepared ahead of time, usually consisting of potato salad and boiled ham or chicken, and pie or cake.

They also enjoyed camp meetings that lasted a week. Those who had tents cooked meals and invited others to eat with them. After they moved to Dakota they attended camp meetings in Nebraska, crossing the river at Yankton in a small boat as there was no ferry.

Written by Hulda Erdmann Repstein, January 1952

## Anna Kretchmer Rother
## Beadle County
## 1889

Once upon a time—to be specific September 24, 1864, in a little village called Pohlsdorf not far distant from the city of Breslau in the province of Silesia, Germany, a little girl was born to Anton (a tenant farmer) and Josepha Sauer Kretschmer. She was christened "Anna Pauline Augusta" for her three godparents at the time of her baptism. The name "Pauline" was for her mother's sister "Pauline Sauer", the same Pauline Sauer with whom Joseph Rother [her future husband] came to America.

It was the custom of the time to name a child for his or her sponsors in baptism—thus it happened that two of her brothers had the same sponsors, hence the same names, only reversed: Franz Karl Anton, the youngest, who was called Anthony ("Tony"), came to America and lived in Huron until the time of his death; and Anton Karl Franz—Frank Kretchmer of Tracy, Minnesota. The "s" was dropped from the name Kretschmer upon coming to America. Anna's third brother Paul remained in Germany and was a baker in Burg near Magdeburg.

When Anna was twelve years old, her mother died and she went to live with a teacher in Polznitz, a nearby village. Her father remarried the daughter of a blacksmith, Rosalie Scharfenberg, of Polznitz, County of Neumarkt. To this union two children were born. The family came to Huron in 1893 and lived on the Rother farm seven miles south of Huron for many years.

Anna suffered from inflammatory rheumatism and each year would have to spend a number of weeks in the hospital. Her doctor told her if she could ever cross the Atlantic Ocean she would not be troubled with that affliction again, so arrangements were made in 1889 for her to come and live with her uncle, C.A. Sauer, in Huron. Strange as it may seem, she never had inflammatory rheumatism again. What spot in the ocean it was that cured her (if there was one) will always remain a mystery.

Her uncle's home was a very busy one with five children. Another child was born in January of 1895, after Anna was married, but he lived only a month. Besides the Sauer home, there was a large rooming house next door which required a great deal of laundry and cleaning, so Anna was seldom idle.

However, she did have occasion to learn to know Joseph Rother who often called at the Sauer residence. [He had come to America in this way:] It so happened that a distant relative of his, Pauline Sauer, was leaving to visit her brothers in America, so he booked passage on the same ship which left Germany the early part of 1888 and came with her to "The Promised Land." After a long and stormy journey, they arrived in Baltimore on February 22. The flags were flying and Joseph thought America was really giving him a royal welcome; however, he learned later it was George Washington's birthday that was being celebrated.

Anna had often heard about Joseph. In fact, she had visited in his home in Zangwitz but had never before met him as he had always been away at school at the time of her visits.

A romance developed and the date for the wedding was set. In those days, it was not customary to wear a white wedding dress, so Anna had a lovely red dress made but "Auntie Sauer" (as Anna always called Mrs. C.A. Sauer), frowned upon the idea of a red wedding dress. "Married in red, you'll wish yourself dead." So Anna bought green material, but Auntie again was not in favor of that color, saying, "Married in green, not fit to be seen," but "married in blue, he'll always be true." So blue material in an embossed design was finally secured and made up for the occasion.

The skirt was plain in the front and flared at the back. The blouse was tight-fitting with a blue and gold changeable taffeta vest or front and a shirred high collar of the same material fastened in the back. Her tan hat was what is now called "Princess Eugenie" style – a very small round crown which tapered down into an elongated shape rather pointed at the front and the back. This was edged in blue velvet to match her dress and trimmed in blue velvet ribbon and tiny plumes of a light beige color. She must have made a very sweet-looking little bride. Her hair was a reddish brown and she wore bangs.

After the wedding ceremony and a wedding dinner at the Sauer home, they left for Volga for their "Honeymoon Cottage."

"Joseph loved music and while in Volga became a part of a musical group who used to sing "Old Black Joe" to him because he was in charge of the coal house. When he brought his bride to Volga, of course, they had to charivari the newly married couple and the band brought six kitchen chairs as a wedding gift. Some of the group came from as far distant as ten miles to take part in the festivities.

A bill of sale for some of the Rother's first furniture from L. M. Kenyon dated October 12, 1892, reads as follows:

| | |
|---|---:|
| One Bedroom Suite | $20.00 |
| One Spring | 3.00 |
| One Mattress | 4.00 |
| One Couch | 16.00 |
| One Center Table | 4.00 |
| Three Chairs Cain | 6.00 |
| One Rocker | 3.00 |
| Three Curtains | 2.10 |
| | $58.10 |

Since Joseph was earning only $40.00 a month, it took more than a month's salary to pay for even these few items.

After only a few months in Volga, Joseph was transferred back to Huron as a trucker and car checker and lived only a short distance from where Joseph worked for the Chicago and Northwestern Railway.

Such menial labor for one so highly educated as Joseph was! It was the custom for one son in a family to study for the priesthood in the Roman Catholic church. Accordingly, when Joseph was twelve years old, he had been sent to Breslau to further his education.

In addition to his training as an Altar Boy and singing in the choir, he could speak seven different languages fluently. Upon his graduation from Gymnasium or the University of Breslau in 1877, because there was so much unrest between Church and State, Joseph had chosen not to enter the priesthood but, instead, became a teacher and for ten years taught in Eastern Germany and Krakau, Poland. The people there were very poor and the future not too promising, so he decided to do what so many young men of his time were doing — seek his fortune in America.

What a struggle it must have been for the young couple. There were so many things for Anna to take care of since Joseph worked nights when the children were small. The home had to be kept quiet during the day so Joseph could sleep. The children had to be cared for and the many household duties attended to, such as cooking, baking, washing, ironing, sewing, mending, etc. Besides taking care of the chickens, milking the cow, and having a big garden to provide food for the family table, as there were no deep-freezers or commercially canned vegetables in those days.

Joseph retired from the railroad in November, 1924, and they had planned upon his retirement to buy a small new home and had saved all through the years for just that purpose. However, in January of 1924 the banks closed, wiping out all their nestegg and the dream house never became a reality.

## SCANDINAVIANS

"To the people of Europe where the high price of real estate confers distinction upon its owner, it seems beyond belief that the United States should give to each individual asking for it, one hundred sixty acres of land." So began one of the "boomer" tracts that drew settlers by the thousands to the land of milk and honey in Dakota.

The word was broadcast throughout the world in a hundred languages, by newspaper ads and pamphlets, touring railroad exhibits and through paid agents: "Uncle Sam is rich enough to give us all a farm."

To Helen Bergh's ancestors in rockbound and mountainous Norway, this was a dream of a better life. "Norway didn't have the land," she explains. "There was no place for young people to spread out. A boy of fourteen could only go to sea," Helen continues. "My uncle was gone four years to sea. In a violent storm, the captain came up to him with a rope with a big old knot in it. 'You'll take the sails down or taste this,' he threatened. Faced with a choice between a beating or drowning, my uncle climbed up and took down the sails."

"We are a stern, forbidding lot," Helen laughs. "I come from stock that found life hard. My grandpa worked in a shipyard, putting rivets into the hulls of ships, for forty years. He had to pound them so they came to a little peak or the ship would leak. One shoulder was up, and one down from that work. One of the babies that Grandpa and Grandma lost, they wouldn't let Grandpa have time off from the shipyard to go to the funeral."

The women always worked, in the home in Norway and the fields in America. "I have my dad's mother's spinning wheel, and I think of all the thousands of miles of yarn that spinning wheel must have spun," Helen reflects.

Another of Helen's prize possessions is her Grandmother Larsen's worn steel thimble, with which she hand-sewed the heavy oilskin coats for the fishermen in the family. To Helen, this thimble speaks of her grandmother's "initiative and industry, and the fact that she probably worked twenty out of twenty-four hours."

Grandmother Larsen had a home bakery. Early every morning she started the fire in the large brick oven which was several feet across. She'd swab out the ashes, and when the bricks were hot, she would put the loaves of bread on a paddle and pop them onto the floor of the oven where they'd bake to a golden brown. Little Susanna (Helen's mother) would deliver them to the neighbors still hot.

An extremely bright woman with a marvelous sense of humor, Grandma Larsen never learned to speak English. "She was fifty-three when she came to this country," Helen explains. "That's too old to pioneer."

The family began to lose the language. Helen's older brother could speak with their grandparents, but they both died when Helen was very young. "There was no reason to talk Norwegian except at Christmas time when everything was a deep, dark secret," she chuckles.

Hard and endless work continued once the family came to the States. "But no matter how bad it got here," Helen says, "it wasn't as bad as it was at home." Among the papers she has saved is a cancelled mortgage for a hay rake her father bought for $40.00. The interest was 12% and there was a mortgage not only on the machine, but also on their spotted calf. "I'll always remember my dad coming in the evening, a role of binder canvas on his back, singing, 'Work for the night is coming, when man's work is over.'" The irony may have escaped him, but not his daughter.

The Norwegians were the earliest and largest foreign-born group in South Dakota in the 1850's. By the 1910 census they made up the second largest ethnic group in South Dakota, close behind the Germans. Ten years later, Norwegians were again the largest foreign-born population in the state, followed by Germans and Russians. Norwegians far surpassed other Scandinavian settlers; there were only half as many Swedes and a third as many Danes.

Many of these Scandinavian homesteaders were drawn from the old settlements in southeastern Minnesota and western Wisconsin by the seductive land agents working for the territorial government or the railroads. They came, not as individuals, but as families and settlements.

The families from the old country often came in steps. One son would come over and scout around until he found land like that at home. He'd work until he had enough money to send for another family member, who would come over and help the next one to make the trip, until finally the whole family was in the new country. By the turn of the century, about a third of Scandinavian immigrants traveled on tickets which had been prepaid.

Later they educated their children (generally the sons) in the same way. If they could get the money to educate the oldest son, he would help the next one, and so on, each one helping the next. "Use one hand to wash the other," Helen's mother used to say.

It was not easy in the new country. In one of the account books Helen's father kept, he totaled up what he was worth after twenty-five years in America. It came to $2500.00. "Any hobo could have done as well and not have had to work as hard, either," was his wry comment.

"Our heritage from these pioneer ancestors," Helen maintains, "is courage and stick-to-it-tiveness. We can't imagine the privations they suffered. They had patience, a dream, and the optimism that 'next year is going to be better.'"

## Susanna Larsen Bergh
## Brown County
## 1881

Agents working in Drammen, Norway back in 1881 advertised South Dakota as a Utopia. My father, Gunder Larsen, was impressed with the tales of gold and beauties of the far-off land. In April of 1881, I found myself on a combination sail and steamship. As the "Kate" left the shores of Norway, we Larsens—seven in all—began wondering about our new life. Three weeks later we immigrants were herded off to Castle Gardens, New York. I can still remember the ladies dressed in fine silks and satins coming to watch us disembark.

Back in early 1881, the train stopped in Groton, South Dakota, since the rails hadn't reached Aberdeen, which then boasted only one shanty. [We came] to the Kristen Andersen home, five miles northwest of Aberdeen. Our home for six weeks was a tent near their house. Each night we made a smudge to smoke out the mosquitoes so that we could sleep. During this time, my father was building a frame house and digging a well. Ma hauled the dirt out of the well and helped bank the house with sod.

Whenever Pa went to Aberdeen, he would take his knife and cut clumps of grass as a trail marker to find his way home. He cut his hay with a scythe and the women folk used hand rakes. Before the summer ended, he had his first team of oxen.

The men, during their spare time, would gather up buffalo bones and stones and haul them by wagonloads to Aberdeen. The bones were shipped east to be ground up for fertilizer and the stones used for buildings.

August of 1881 was a never-to-be-forgotten month. An eight year old can stretch his ears to hear most everything and the tales of prairie fires ran tingles down my back. Early one morning, Pa saw a wisp of smoke to the northwest. A brisk wind was blowing so the family began making a

Susanna Larsen Bergh

path around the haystack. We all hauled sand from the well to lay on the path. The house was surrounded with clay from the cellar so the well water was poured on the sand path. As the sky became redder, I was sent to the house while the others hurried across the ravine to take down a wooden calf pen. This precious lumber had to be saved. Our cattle pulled their ropes free to run to a little patch of plowed ground. It was thought that locators might have become careless and started the fire. More prairie fires followed but this one scared me the most.

Aberdeen, in the meantime, had its first railroad – the Milwaukee. It came on July 5th. Leonard, my brother, helped lay the tracks from Groton onward. The town plat began to materialize into buildings.

Spring of 1882 gladdened even the heart of a homesick Norwegian girl. The fire-blackened ground burst forth with multi-colored shades of green dotted with all shades of flowers; crocuses and violets, buttercups, and later the anemones, wild geraniums and the pink roses. Nature was at her loveliest. Herding the cows amidst this wild beauty was a delight until I found underneath the tall grasses snakes and badger holes. And how thrilling it was to stand still and listen to the call of the prairie hens and the songs of the meadowlarks.

During the summer of 1882, I saw my first threshing machine, a horse powered affair. It had no blower and as Ma cut the straw bands, the bundle feeders threw in the grain. While one man kept the horses going, another sacked the grain. Then Pa (who was sixty-one) and Leonard hauled the grain to Columbia by wagon to be milled. They left by early morning moonlight and I sat outdoors at night listening for the click of the iron wheels. That same year, Pa and Leonard walked the twenty miles to Columbia to buy two cows. This was in July and Pa wore his derby. Coming back Pa became so hot and sickish that Leonard milked one of the cows and gave him milk to drink from his derby.

Indian scares were common, although never a reality. And whenever there was sickness, neighbors offered their services.

Little Susanna was growing up. On April 4th of 1893 I was married to Andrew Hans Bergh in a marriage which lasted until July 16th, 1921. Through these years we watched our town grow, a school expand, lyceums turning into a Community Club.

Today finds me ready to celebrate my seventy-sixth birthday, an active member in my community and a woman interested in the affairs of not only her country but the world at large.

# Nellie Proper Beachem Hunstad
## Brown County
## 1880

In the spring of 1880, a small group of Norwegians who lived some twenty miles north of the capital of Norway, Oslo, sold all their interests in their native land and purchased tickets to Watertown, Dakota Territory. Watertown was the end of rail service. They knew of the government plan of homesteading and planned to establish new homes in this far-away land.

Among the group were Mr. and Mrs. Ole Hunstad and their two sons, who brought their brides-to-be with them. Nils Hunstad had made a trip to the U.S. two years earlier and had worked on farms in Minnesota. He had been instructed to advise his parents as to the conditions in this new land and if they desired, they were to follow. He, however, returned to Norway, feeling that he would like to make the move but realized that the move must be up to them.

One can hardly realize the hours of planning, the discussions necessary, the decisions as to what to sell and what to bring along, the heartaches caused by leaving friends and relatives, and parting with the things and places of which they were so fond, the anticipation of a fuller life in the new land and fear of defeat in the new venture.

Out of this train of thought, we realize that the timid stayed behind while the more courageous were found among the passengers on the first steamship lines that plied the Atlantic, bringing their cargo of people to settle this vast new country.

The ship that carried the group landed safely in New York Harbor thirty-some days after leaving Oslo. It was several days late due to heavy seas. I have no record of the train service but some of the baggage was lost and broken in transit.

When they arrived in Watertown, quarters had to be established where most of the group could stay while their men, including Nils Hunstad, set out on horseback to locate a place suitable for homesteading. Fertile land and water was a must. They also kept in mind that the group wanted land joining and if possible, other relatives and friends might follow.

Not many homesteaders took advantage of the liberal free land offered by the government but it was possible to acquire a quarter section of land each. That made a sizable piece of land in one area.

The three men rode in a northerly direction from Watertown. They reached a point somewhere near what is Waubay. They then turned west and came to the James River. The spring runoff had caused the river to overflow its banks. The whole river flat was covered with water. They thought they had reached a huge river.

They marked several places in their map which they thought suitable and returned to Watertown. Their trip gained them nothing since in each place they had marked off, some other party had filed on some of the land so the group could not get their land together.

With the help of the government land office, they all filed on land which was west of the James River and north of the Moccasin Creek. There were no bridges and the land not easily accessible.

Then began the task of moving. Purchases had to be made—oxen, wagons and supplies. A group started out with a wagon and four oxen hauling lumber. Nils and Edward were in this group while others stayed to tend to the purchasing. They wanted to erect a sod shanty on the land on which they had filed.

When the first shanty had been built, Edward, who was nineteen years old, was left to care for the oxen and break up more sod for the shanties while the others returned to Watertown on horseback. They supposed they had left enough food to keep him until they got back, but more time was required than they had planned and when the wagon train had finally crossed the James River, the group decided to camp for the night before crossing the Moccasin Creek where it empties into the James River. That evening some of the men rode across on horseback and when they arrived at the newly built cabin, they found Ed had run out of food except for a few potatoes and that a bolt of lightning had killed one of his oxen.

One reason the wagon train was overdue was the fact that the unsuspecting newcomers had bought several oxen which had never been broken for driving. One can imagine the confusion caused when an ox wanted a drink and headed for a waterhole, taking the wagon with him.

Each homesteader received from the government free packages of garden seeds. The seeds were planted in the newly broken soil but the newcomers did not know what would come up and, in many instances, did not know what to do with the vegetables since they were not familiar with them. Huge watermelons grew on the fertile land but the women tried without success to cook them in various ways and ended up by feeding them to the cattle.

# Marie Holstad
# Brown County
# 1893

Because their mother had courage, three little boys grew to manhood in the United States and received the heritage of American citizenship. That pioneer mother is Mrs. Marie B. Holstad.

It was in 1893 that a young Norwegian Miss disembarked from the vessel which had carried her from Norway to Canada and traveled by train to the prairie town of Aberdeen, South Dakota.

Aberdeen in the spring of 1893 presented a dismal picture of flooded streets, board sidewalks and mud, according to Mrs. Holstad, who was welcomed to the village by her prospective husband, Bendick Holstad, who had been her classmate in Norway. He had come to America nine years earlier.

That year the first Bethlehem Lutheran Church was under construction and so the young couple was married in a little house on the site of the present Civic Arena. It was in this little house that they made their first home.

Three sons were born to the couple. Mr. Holstad was a bookbinder and an employee of the American-News Printing Company. He was also the first organist in Bethlehem Lutheran church.

Tragedy struck the immigrant family when the father became ill, died, and left his young wife and three small sons, the oldest, four, and the youngest, six months. Almost penniless and unable to speak the language of her adopted country, Mrs. Holstad was faced with a momentous decision. Should she return to Norway where her brother promised to build a home for her family, or should she remain in Aberdeen?

Little Mrs. Holstad (she's only four feet, seven inches tall) recalled the rigorous life of her seafaring relatives in

Norway and the difficulty with which they paid for an education. Her decision was made. She would remain in America. Her sons would not grow up to sail the sea and they would have opportunity for an education.

Life was not easy for the brave little woman who found herself the sole support of three growing boys. Perhaps one of her greatest handicaps was her inability to speak English and so, unaided, Mrs. Holstad taught herself to speak, read and write the language of her adopted country. She worked wherever honest work was to be found.

The three little boys grew to manhood and with the years helped lighten their mother's burdens. Nowadays the frail little woman putters about the house, waters her plants and on bright days enjoys South Dakota sunshine in a lawn chair. Failing eyesight has forced her to give up reading, but she listens with keen interest and understanding to radio programs and newscasts. Sundays finds the alert little pioneer mother near her radio listening to broadcasts from the Bethlehem Lutheran and other churches.

by Carolyn Stone

Ingeborg Aakar Simons

## Ingeborg Aaker Simons
## Minnehaha County
## 1877

Life was a precious, exhilarating experience for my grandmother, Ingeborg Aaker Simons. Every moment was filled with the expectancy of useful or pleasant endeavor, whether it was her moments of physical activity as she performed the duties of managing the farm and the family while her husband was away, or her spiritual moments spent in worship or those precious bits of time spent in contemplative silence as she strolled through the old apple orchard humming a song to herself. Indeed, time was valuable to grandmother and not to be wasted and none of it was, even those moments of it that were spent purely for the joy of living. The fruits of the wonderful moments of her eighty-one years were stored in her sympathetic heart and fine, keen mind, one by one.

As was the case with most of the pioneer women of her time, she was by choice as well as by necessity, frugal. She, too, was a "saver" of things. Even small things that might some day be useful, like string, buttons and paper sacks. "Save it for seven years and then if you have no use for it, throw it away," she often exhorted those in her family.

But Grandmother was probably a more ambitious saver of the intangible things — spiritual, intellectual and cultural — and "to lay up treasures in heaven where rust and moth do not corrupt" may be said to have been her true motto in life.

Because she was already well advanced in years in my own first memories of her, I visualize her as she sat at the more sedentary tasks which were usually hers by virtue of years, such as paring the vegetables or weaving the rugs. Often as she sat occupied with some humble work she would draw from the wealth stored in her mind a fascinating story or a memorized hymn, which she taught to others who were more actively engaged in washing the dishes or kneading the bread. Many times an open hymn book was at her side as they would learn a new song together. To be sure, the song was sung so that the melody as well as the words were learned, for Grandmother had come rightly by her love and appreciation of music. From her mother she had apparently inherited this tendency and also some of the other talents she exhibited.

Her mother, Aslaug Gunleiksdatter Moen, was said by an old family story to have been a singer, artistic weaver and a nurse. Her father was Ole Drengmanson Aaker. They were of Norwegian descent and lived on the mountainous slopes near Hjartdal, Telmarken, Norway, where their family of seven children were born.

Grandmother was very fond of her closest sister, Margit, and they played together on the steep slopes near their home by a cascading stream. Margit wore a little bell so that the mother could easily locate them as they played. She was called "Margit with the bell."

Some of the descendants of Margaret, as she came to be called in America, include a grandniece, the wife of Dr. J.C.K. Preus, who is secretary of the board of Christian Education of the Evangelical Lutheran Church. One of Mrs. Preus' nieces is the wife of the Reverend Norval Hegland, of the well known "air parish" near Lemmon, South Dakota.

Dr. Preus visited the old family home of the Aakers in Hjartdal in 1936 and found the original two room house still standing. At this time it was well over one hundred years old. "The white washed fireplace standing in the corner, the three wooden benches and the hinged folding table were evidently built when the house was constructed. The old door leading from the front entry had some very old decorations, typical of the Telmarken Kunst. This door was evidently original", wrote Dr. Preus after his visit.

But the confines of this humble dwelling were too small for the Aaker family by 1848 and the little acreage on the mountain side would scarcely support the family, which by this time had increased to its fullest extent and included seven children. This family left their little home in Hjardal, Norway and emigrated to America, the land of opportunity, leaving many friends and relatives behind. At this time the youngest child was two years of age and my grandmother was six. They settled in Muskego, Wisconsin, among many of their countrymen who had arrived before them.

It was while the Aakers were at Muskego that Ingeborg was confirmed into the Lutheran faith by Dr. V. Koren, home mission pastor of the pioneer Muskego church. Her name is recorded on the list of confirmands of that early church which has now been moved from its original location to St. Paul, Minnesota, where it stands as a memorial to the early church pioneers.

In 1854 the Aaker family, having now become better acquainted with this new land, chose to move further westward. They went to Winnesheik County, Iowa, where they established the "Burr Oaks Springs" farm. Ingeborg was twelve at this time. She remained with her family and worked both in the fields and within the home as most young girls did at that time.

She had very little formal schooling, but availed herself of every opportunity and learned to speak and write the English language well, mostly by studying and reading at night.

As she grew into womanhood her inherited ability with a needle developed and she became quite proficient as a seamstress. In later years, her fondness for sewing justified the fact that she was the first in her community to possess a sewing machine and many a dress and petticoat were stitched on this machine, most of the time without any remuneration.

At the family home on "Burr Oaks Springs" Ingeborg had grown into a rather tall, slender girl with smiling blue eyes. She had a quick wit and a ready laugh, which made her pleasant company. She was now seventeen and she had met "the man of her life". His name was John Seim. He was twenty-six years old and had come to America from Norway when he was eleven. He, too, loved to learn and had made use of the chance to learn to speak and write the English language from an Irishman for whom he had worked. Their engagement was short, however. It was a characteristic trait of Grandmother that once she had made up her mind, there was no use wasting time, and she was ready to begin this new phase of her life. They were married on November 2, 1859.

They started their new life together on a farm near Ridgeway, Iowa, where they lived for eighteen years with the exception of a period of three and one-half years when Grandfather served in the Union Army of his country fighting the Civil War. Grandmother and her two small sons lived at her parental home during part of this time.

Within the decade following the close of the Civil War, four other children were born. The parents now began to feel the adventurous call of the Dakota Territory. One quarter section of land as a homestead together with another quarter section as a tree claim was a great enticement to make a new home further westward.

It was difficult to pull up stakes in familiar territory, to leave friends and relatives who mourned their departure and to set out for a far away and strange place, but the pioneer spirit was strong and the break was made. They were westward bound! The long trek of about three hundred miles was made by wagon in the summer of 1877. The two youngest children were brought along while the four oldest were left at home to tend the farm and the crops until Grandfather could come back to harvest them.

They settled in Lone Rock township, Moody County, south of Flandreau in what was known as Dakota Territory. Norwegian settlers had already arrived in this locality so they were among congenial people. A two room sod house was quickly constructed. The new dwelling however, could boast of nothing more for a door than a heavy quilt with which to keep out the weather, wild beasts or any undesirable characters.

Such were the circumstances in which Grandmother lived alone with her young children while her husband made the long journey back to their original home in Ridgeway to harvest the crop and settle all his affairs. This accomplished, Grandfather, with the older children, returned to Dakota Territory to take up their new life in a new home. To the John Seim family, 1877 was truly an important year.

Not only did the family have a new home, but very soon they were to adopt a new name as well. They did this as a matter of convenience and not because they were becoming so Americanized that they were ashamed of the Norwegian name and heritage.

A family by the same name as John Seim had settled north of Flandreau and the mail for the two families often became mixed, causing great inconvenience, delay and many disappointments. One day, in great exasperation, Grandfather noticed a name printed on the outside of the blacksmith shop. "There is a fine name for us", he said, "from now on our name will be Simons". And so it was. Whether it was done by legal procedure is not known. However, the problem of mixed mail was solved.

These adjustments having been made, they greeted each new experience with eagerness. They were not unaware that there would be much hard work and many sacrifices, but they had health and strength, courage and a zest for pioneering, and most important, they had a reverence for life and a strong faith in the providence of God. Indeed, they were grateful that their own church had followed them to this new place.

The Norwegian Lutheran Church of Lone Rock was organized by Rev. A.O. Sando in the same year that the Simons family had come to make their home in that new territory and they, ever feeling the need for constant spiritual guidance and associations, were among the charter members.

Grandmother very quickly adjusted herself to the new life on the Dakota prairies and its many duties because she was energetic and progressive. She was intelligent and a great reader. She had an exceptionally hospitable nature and good fun was one of her delights, though by nature she was serious minded. She was not afraid of hard work and was blessed with the strength and health that it required. She had a fine ability for leadership in church and community affairs. She was able to express herself before others and had the courage to stand up for what she believed was right. She did not hesitate to face problems squarely. Though she had a certain firmness about her character, she always settled her difficulties with all fairness and with consideration for others.

Ingeborg Simons loved God's Word, her church and its mission program and she had an unusual love for people. She was aware of the fact that her life and all other lives were precious in the sight of God. Truly, Grandmother had a high regard for life and the privilege of living.

A circumstance, besides her own conviction, that may have accounted for her intense interest in spiritual things was the fact that two of her nieces, daughters of her sister, Margaret, were married to ministers. These relatives were very close to Grandmother because they were the daughters of her favorite sister. Often they came to visit and many an interesting theological discussion was carried on at the Simons' during these visits.

She was generous, too, perhaps some would say, almost to a fault. It may be that this characteristic accounted for the fact that during her long life of eighty-one years, she probably stored up more treasures in heaven than in the local bank, though there was always the air of fine and comfortable living which pervaded the home. Somehow, an indefinable quality of warm hospitality and fun prevailed, which made being there pleasant and interesting.

It was her belief that the members of the family should be encouraged to bring their friends home at any time, where simple good times were encouraged. Because Grandmother was so sincerely friendly, she attracted not only the staid older folks, but more especially the friends of her children. She could enjoy to the fullest, a harmless practical joke, even on herself, or a story well told, and any music was a joy to her. Of course there was always plenty of good, simple food, freely offered. Small wonder that the Simons' home was a favorite gathering place for all.

After coming to Dakota, the family increased by five. There were eleven children. Eventually all married except the oldest son.

The necessity of education for her large brood was a matter of grave concern to Grandmother. She knew so well that the written word could open up wide vistas of thought and enjoyment. She herself had struggled for learning, unaided. She wanted her children to have the advantage of an education. So before a school house was provided in Lone Rock township, some classes were held in the two room sod house at Simons'.

It was said that one little girl who came to school was so unusually shy that she would hold her hand up to her face and peek through her fingers. Often, when the little hand was not too clean, Grandmother would wash her hands.

The older children would sometimes tease Martina but Grandmother was her refuge and would not permit them to take unfair advantage of her.

Just as she helped the cause of this shy little pupil in her quest for learning, she also helped the cause of every teacher who ever taught the school district during her lifetime. The teacher nearly always "boarded" at Grandmother's. At one time for eighteen consecutive years, the teacher stayed there. One year she decided to take a rest from this responsibility but within the year, for some reason, the teacher was back at Simons'.

Besides the obvious reasons why the school teachers should be happy at Grandmother's house, another fact was apparent, and this was the predominate use of the English language. Grandmother had come to do most of her reading in English and it was almost a law that this should be the spoken language. She probably insisted on this out of consideration for the many times when non-Norwegians were present in the home. However, the native tongue was not neglected and she made sure that all learned to read and write the Norwegian. Evidently this close contact with the school and its teachers through the years influenced several members of the household to enter the teaching profession. It is my belief that Grandmother, herself, was a wonderful teacher.

She might also have been a nurse, for she had a flair for helping the sick. In the neighborhood many a newborn infant was welcomed into the world with only Mrs. Simons to greet it. In those days, too, epidemics would often run rampant and she was called many times to help nurse neighbors and friends back to health. Grandfather would also lend a willing hand with farm chores if that was most needful. And in some miraculous way her family was always spared at least any severe losses or sickness.

Her interests, however, were not confined to her own immediate affairs or community, but spilled over somewhat into the civic and political realms as well. Because she read a great deal, she was aware of the current problems of her day and followed avidly the progress of the popular trends of the time, such as woman's suffrage and the temperance movements. Her husband, as well, was interested in the political trends of the day.

In 1898 Grandfather died after a period of poor health, leaving his wife to outlive him by a quarter of a century.

In 1901 the new house, which was needed and planned for prior to his death, was built. It was a far cry from the old sod "two rooms with a lean-to over the door" house which had served the family for many years and which had seen births, marriages, church services, school sessions, organization meetings of various sorts and many an important social event and visits from prominent persons.

Miss Katerina Elilie tells that she remembers having spent the night in the Simons' sod house with her father and mother when she was very small. The room was made private by the use of calico curtains. A straw tick was placed on the floor and an extra cot was drawn from beneath another bed. In this way extra persons were often accommodated for the night.

The sod house was the place where the Young People's Society, or the Luther League, as it is know today, was first organized in that community. It was customary at that time to serve the refreshments as a regular meal is served, instead of on trays as we often do today. This, of course, involved a great deal of work. On one of these occasions, countless lemon meringue pies had been made, most of them by the young lady who was engaged to my Uncle Albert, and one wonders where space could be found in which to store them until serving time.

The Young People's Society grew in numbers and popularity. Some years later, though still in the era of the sod house, a rally was held at which about two hundred people were present. A neighborhood band from another community furnished music. During the afternoon it started to rain, so the crowd went to the barn, which was then new, and played games.

Now a new house had been built. There was plenty of room for meetings and guests, for the new house had nine rooms, an attic, cellar and a large back porch. This is the house that holds many memories for me as, in my mind, I wander through it once again. There was the living room. It was furnished, among other things, with a fascinating couch for resting, a secretary bookcase and a center table. A nice big Uncle sat in a big chair where he smoked while he read the paper in the evening and Grandma rocked in the little rocker in which she had in the past soothed many tired babies to sleep.

The dining room was unadorned except for the long table, covered with a cloth. There was a large picture on the wall. A built-in cupboard stood between the living and dining room instead of in the step-saving location near the kitchen as it would be arranged in the modern home. Possibly the cupboard held only "company" dishes and was placed there because of its attractiveness.

The kitchen was interesting to me only because it was the source of the good food, that is all except the delicious bread which came from the old copper boiler in the depths of the cool basement when it was time for a meal to be served. What delicious bread! Grandmother had taught her girls of "both her families" to master well the old black cook stove in the corner of the kitchen. As a sign that this was a "modern house", there was a cistern pump which furnished the running water and a drain into a septic tank, an unusual convenience in that day.

I remember Grandma very little in connection with the work in the kitchen, for she had turned this over to the young who had been her apprentices. Still, here she had taught more than the practical arts, for she had given a course in the appreciation of the spiritual and the cultural things, in the time that might have been wasted, while at the same time, entertaining as well as teaching her young helpers.

The same year that the new Simons house was built, another wonderful dream came true. The Lone Rock Lutheran Church was built. Rev. J.A. Blilie, who had come in 1880 to labor in this vast field, had now realized some of the fruits of his labors. Now, it would no longer be necessary to hold church services in the homes or the school. However, the pastor had a large area to serve and it was not possible to have services every Sunday. On those Sundays when formal church services were not held, it was the custom of Grandmother to have a sort of worship service for her own family at home. There would be a regular sermon from a book of sermons and there would be hymns and prayers. Sunday was the Sabbath day whether the pastor could be present or not.

The first funeral from the new church was one which affected Grandmother's life, for it was that of her own son's wife. She had died in childbirth, leaving three small children. The new home had barely been initiated when she took this second family of young ones into her home and heart to guide and care for. In view of the unfortunate death, there was still much to be thankful for, since Grandmother was still able to care for them and give them the love that compared favorably with that they would have had from their own dear mother. On the other hand, the son, Ole, was able to take over the responsibility of the farm. This satisfactory arrangement continued until the children were well on their own. The wonderful love and care that she gave to these children, her second family, has never been forgotten by them.

These children, who were my cousins, were adults when I first began to be conscious of Grandmother's character and influence. Now the house, no longer new, was permeated not only by Grandmother's influence alone, but also by an intangible feeling of faith and peace and order which she had managed to instill in those of her household. A wonderful heritage she has given! But there is still more of the house to be seen. There is Grandma's own room. It is so much like her, cozy, warm, interesting and neat. Here was her sanctuary, to which she retired later in the evening to read her devotional book and whatever other reading struck her fancy.

In one or two of the other bedrooms there were bookcases filled with books. It was here that I cried over the mistreatment of "Black Beauty" and thrilled to the joys and sorrows of "Little Women". Grandmother was passing on to the third generation a love for good reading.

The attic, wonder of wonders, was reached by a mysterious ladder that folded up out of sight. Here there were trunks and chests of outgrown clothing and toys and neatly stacked papers being "saved for seven years". The old scroll upon which the Bible pictures and stories could be turned like a moving picture, was kept up there now since the young ones of the household had outgrown that mode of story telling. With a little coaxing, Grandma would once again assume her loved role as teacher of the gospel story and she would turn the pictures of the scroll for the benefit of wide-eyed grandchildren.

There was, of course, a guest bedroom downstairs with which I wasn't much concerned. But the parlor! It was in this room where a strange and noisy mixture of Norwegian and English languages literally buzzed when Grandmother served the Ladies Aid. There stood the piano which had been purchased after the musician of the family, my mother, had learned to play "Rustle of Spring" on the family organ. From then on, it was my mother's part-time occupation, at least, to drive over the countryside with horse and buggy, teaching music to whatever child aspired to become a musician. It was not such a strange coincidence then, that she also visited regularly my husband's parental home, where he, as a little boy, hid bashfully behind his mother's voluminous and protective skirts.

All of this and Grandma's love for the great outdoors has not been told. Was this communion also one of the sources of her mellow personality? I used to walk with her. To me it seemed those quiet walks through the orchard were filled with a sort of worship. And was it from her that I, too, learned to love the outdoors with its trees and flowers, grass and good, black dirt? She used to pick up the sticks that would fall from the trees so that the yard would look neat. She used to stoop and gather in her full apron the wind-fall apples, that they should not be wasted. The pungent smell of apples ripening on the back porch seemed to fill the room as they awaited the preserving kettle and a hot fire in the kitchen stove. Today the sweet smell of apples anywhere seems to belong to Grandma just as much as the little phrase of endearment which she always saved especially for the little people she loved, "sweetie, honey, darlin'."

A year or so before her death, when it no longer was advisable for her to remain on the farm, she moved into Flandreau where she lived with my mother until her death at the age of eighty-one years. She was spared any long or severe illness, but died after a siege of pneumonia. She is buried in the Lone Rock Cemetery, near the neighbors, friends and relatives who were so dear to her.

So closed a noble life, not especially spectacular in its accomplishments, nevertheless, potent in its influence on many lives that touched hers. She had worked and worshipped, loved and given of herself, and the treasures which she had lived to store were left in the hearts and minds of those whom she knew and loved, as an enduring inheritance.

# Kristianna Sigdestad Olson
## Day County
## 1889

Kristianna Sigdestad was born in 1861 in Opstryn, Nordfjord, Norway; she was baptized and confirmed in the Lutheran faith in Norway. In this beautiful country with its valleys, fjords, mountains, and waterfalls, she spent her childhood. My mother had the privilege of attending the school on the location where they lived on the "gaard" Sigdestad. Being children of humble peasants it became their lot in early life to leave home and work for their living. This was rugged and often my mother would tell of how hard she was compelled to work for her master where she milked cows and made cheese products. Her food was portioned for a certain time and often this was not sufficient to quench the hunger of a growing teenager. She would be so hungry she would go to bed weary, hungry and weeping. These trials made her resolve in early years to try her luck in America.

At the age of eighteen she emigrated to America with a cousin, Rasmus Mark, arriving in Montevideo, Minnesota the summer of 1880. She was the first of her family to leave her native land.

She went to work in the family of a storekeeper in Montevideo for the sum of $1.00 a week, I think. They were a large family, but work did not prove more difficult than what she had been accustomed to. One advantage was that the family was unable to speak the Norwegian language, so Mother just had to learn theirs.

September 5, 1881, she was married to Magnus Olson. They moved to a rented farm between Montevideo and Granite Falls, Minnesota, where they lived until 1889.

Soon they learned that sections of Montana were open to homesteaders, so in the spring of 1889 they gathered their belongings and with their four children in a covered wagon, drawn by a team of horses, and one cow tied behind the wagon, they started out for what they thought their destination would be, Montana.

Mother's parents and two sisters had settled in Dakota Territory the year before and on their way they planned to visit and rest a few days with them. They had located in Day County, about seven miles north of Bristol. The family prevailed on them to go no farther but locate here. The homesteads were all taken but arrangements were made by Dad to buy a quarter section of land three miles east of Grandma Sigdestad. Here in a one-room frame house life was begun anew. A well was drilled by my father which proved a godsend, for this well furnished water for the entire community and steam threshing machines. Today, the well is in good condition and supplying water.

The land was new, crops yielded plentifully, new hope was instilled, and with each year, improved. It was not unusual to see buffalo herds cross the prairie, but with settlers moving in they soon were either killed or moved on.

The prairie fires were the general worry. The winters were severe and blizzards would last for days with snow and bitter cold.

Another quarter section of land was bought adjoining the one they had. Here we have the trading of one of the horses for a team of oxen because the oxen were easier keepers on the forage afforded and for field work proved as satisfactory.

The usual hardships in pioneering were encountered but their courage never failed them; they were schooled in privations.

Soon community life improved, churches were organized. Dad, being a stone mason by trade, laid the first foundation of Bergen Church, his labor donated to a worthy cause, which proves they were much concerned about the welfare of the coming generation, a commendable spirit.

Nine children blessed this home. A new home was partly complete when my father died suddenly January 5, 1898, just thirteen days before my youngest sister was born.

Then Mother shouldered the work of rearing her family, managing the farm and, with limited means, much ambition and labor, she proved successful. Her interest in the affairs of church and schools and the activities of community affairs were constant. Her main concern was her family, which she struggled to prepare to meet the trials of life. Her perseverance and abounding faith in her Lord and Master was ever sufficient.

Contributed by Selma Flakall, a daughter

Ole Warren family

## Rasmene Vanelven Warren and Anna Warren Peart
## Moody County
## 1878

Mother was born in Norway in 1833 and baptized Rasmene Nekoline Nelson, Aaro Vanelven. When she was fourteen years of age she had to leave home to make her own living. Her wages the first year were fifty cents a year together with clothing and necessities. Later when she had learned to spin, weave, knit and make clothing she was paid $1.50 a year. Even on this meager salary she was able to save money enough to pay for her trip to America so on May 14, 1871, she left Norway from Bergen on the sailship "Argo." On that same ship was twenty-seven year old Ole Warren, to whom she was engaged.

While at sea there was a terrific storm, so bad that the captain did not expect anyone to survive, although the passengers slept through it, not realizing the danger. Another event of interest was the birth of two babies, a boy and a girl. The girl was named Argo after the ship, but the boy died and was buried at sea. I remember Mother telling how he was wrapped in a sail and lowered into the ocean.

They arrived at Quebec, Canada, having spent six weeks and one day on the ocean. On July 4th, they arrived in Green Bay, Wisconsin. After a few days of rest Mother began work at a boarding house at fifty cents a week; later she found employment at $1.50 a week. That October she was married to Ole Warren.

Father and Mother shared their first home in Green Bay, Wisconsin, with the couple who was married the same evening and in the same Lutheran Church as they were.

I remember so well how Father used to tell of his early childhood. He was born in 1844, on the place called Warren in Sandro Sondmore, Norway. His parents were Ole Madsen and Gertrude Johanesson. His father died when he was three years old but his Mother was able to take care of him until he was eight years old when he had to leave home and shift for himself. At his first place of employment Father suffered from lack of both food and clothing. His little feet made bloody imprints upon the ground as he herded cattle in the cold.

While my parents were living at Green Bay, Wisconsin, brother John was born; the twin girl was still born. I was also born in Green Bay. In 1873, Father bought eighty acres of timber land at $2.00 an acre. After clearing three or four acres of land, building a log house and a large log barn, Father found that he had to look for work elsewhere so that he could provide for his wife and family. This he found at New Denmark, seven miles from home, where he worked for Fred Rasmusson.

It was during Father's absence that a forest fire broke out and completely ruined our home. Mother rolled our bedding and clothing in a bundle and threw them in a nearby well, hoping later to come and rescue them but even some of these burned. Mother packed our good books and a few baby clothes in a small chest she had brought from Norway. This she carried under her arm as we found shelter in a nearby swamp. It was late on a Sunday afternoon that Father got word that a forest fire was threatening his home. He wanted to start out on foot but kind Mr. Rasmussen persuaded him to wait until after supper then he would take him with the old gray horse and the buckboard. Father told how they had to stop and put out the fire which had started on the horse and the buggy as they drove through the burning timbers. They reached within three-fourth mile of our home and there at the farther end of the swamp, Father found his wife and two children together huddled in the swamp safely. His home had been destroyed but his family was safe and Father said, "God had been good to him and would continue to be good to him."

Mr. Rasmussen took us all to his home. He didn't have much house room but he did have much heart room. It was on August 5 that our home burned and eight days later, my brother Frederick was born. He was baptized while we were there and was named Frederick after the kind Fred Rasmussen who had befriended us. We spent three good months there.

In October we moved back where our home was and lived with one of our neighbors. Again Father started to clean up the place and get ready to build. In December, Knute Mosby came to visit his brother, where we were living. He had been in Dakota Territory and told about what a wonderful place Dakota was and how people could live and farm that nice prairie land without the hard work of clearing and grubbing. Houses were built of sod and hay was used for fuel. Father was interested but it was not until March that he left for South Dakota. Father's traveling bag was a grain sack strapped to his shoulder. And he carried a gun, an old musket from the Civil War.

A friend joined him and the two started out together for the west. After much walking and little riding the two reached Flandreau, South Dakota. There was no place to stay, the small hotel was filled to the brim. So they bought a few crackers and some water for tea (for which they paid thirty-five cents), found a hay stack on the corner across from what is now St. Vincent Hotel, dug a hole, crawled in and expected to spend the night but they found it too crowded as a third prospector had joined them by now. They each grabbed an armful of hay and walked to the river bank, (Sioux) where they found some wagon boxes and there made their bed for the night. That was Father's first night spent in South Dakota.

The next morning they met four others who had come to Dakota for the same purpose. They were now seven in the group. These seven each filed on a quarter of land in the neighborhood which later came to be known as Norwegian Valley located about fifteen miles west of Flandreau. This was on March 29, 1878, and to celebrate this occasion they ate their noon meal together of crackers and slough water out of Lars Pedersen's place.

The following morning Father and Paulson started on foot for Sioux Falls to look for work, father carrying his traveling bag and gun. Before they reached Sioux Falls they had received the answers many times which were so common to foreigners at that time: "No food or lodging for tramps." They even enjoyed the little left of their lunch which they had brought from Wisconsin, a little bread, butter and two hard-boiled eggs. It was too weeks old but better than nothing with slough water to drink.

Father told of how after getting good and tired of being refused food and lodging that he made up his mind that at the next stop, they would stay overnight and he told the farmer as much. Father was amused to hear the farmer tell his wife that the man carrying the gun says he isn't going any farther tonight. The wife gave a demonstrative "no," but Father saved the day when he spoke up in good Norwegian, "I see you are Norwegians, too." That turned the trick, then there was hospitality aplenty. The next morning upon leaving, Father asked the farmer's wife how much they owed her and she wondered if fifteen cents apiece was too much. Father paid her forty cents for the two of them.

Father was handy with tools so he got work with a carpenter-farmer who lived near Sioux Falls. Father worked there most of the time until we moved to our permanent home. Every month Father would have to go back to his homestead and live there a few days, that was necessary according to filing agreements so that Father could rightfully claim his quarter. In the meantime Father had built a good sod house on the homestead.

June 22, 1878, was a memorable day in my life for then Mother, John, Fred and I arrived in Canby, Minnesota. The next morning Father came to get us, driving Knut Severson's sturdy oxen and wagon. That night we slept out in the open under South Dakota's beautiful starry skies on the river bank near Medary. Mother and we three children stayed with the Seversons for three weeks then Father had found a home for us near where he was working. We lived in a small house the owners had built and I can remember the good butter Mother made.

A very sad thing happened to our good friends while we lived there. A terrible storm came up with terrific thunder and lightning. One of their little boys was sitting near an open window, the lightning struck and pulled him halfway out of the window. Of course, it killed him. Mother warned us never to sit near an open window in a storm and a storm never comes up but what I think of it.

By fall we moved to a place where Mother kept house for the owner and that way we saved house rent. He too was very kind to us. He offered Mother half of his potato crop if she would dig all the potatoes. That way we not only got good potatoes but enough to last us until next year.

In February, 1879 we moved to the homestead. Before going, our good friends insisted that Father call on each of the neighbors for food, clothing or items useful in establishing a new household. They furnished the team and wagon and persuaded Father to make the collections. Father said it was one of the hardest things he had ever done, he didn't want to beg. We got some good food and clothing and I especially remember a very pretty pieced quilt which Mother used only on special occasions, for example, on the minister's bed when he came to spend the night with us.

Our good neighbor, Knut Severson, came with his sturdy team of oxen and wagon to haul our household goods to the homestead. But it wasn't without a little trouble for we had a cow and a calf and the cow would not lead tied to the wagon so Father had to walk all the way and lead her. Hans Johnson took Mother and us three children in his covered wagon, The Prairie Schooner, to our new home. It was a long, cold journey.

When we reached the old Deckstader place, which was about halfway, Mr. Johnson stopped to feed his horses and asked if we could come inside to warm up a bit. I can remember yet how cold my feet were in spite of all the good, warm bedding Mother had tucked around us. She held Baby Fred in her arms all the way. Our lunch was almost too cold to eat. Four o'clock that afternoon we arrived at our home, our little sod house. Father had come before us so he had it good and warm for us. We were a happy family, so grateful and thankful that we had this little home all our own. That was February 20, 1879, and today, February 20, 1950, seventy years later, I am writing this story of our family and I am the only one left to tell it.

Our sod house had no floor so when Mother swept she would sprinkle a little water over the black dirt and the scrubbing was done. Father had made our furniture; a bed, a trundle bed for us children and two long benches to sit on. The large chest, which was made in Wisconsin for us to pack our belongings in when we moved to Dakota, served as our table. Later as I grew older the two benches served as my bed. They were pushed together against the wall and my small mattress was filled with straw like the rest of the mattresses, there were no springs or feather beds. The chest was pushed up against the benches so I wouldn't fall out of my bed. We had bought a cook stove in Sioux Falls and nearly all our cooking utensils came with it even to the wash boiler.

Our food the first years consisted mostly of bread and butter, milk and mush. When our cow went dry Mother mixed warm water, syrup and a little vinegar to take the place of milk on our mush. We nearly always had plenty of potatoes and occasionally salt pork but there was not much meat to be had. To supply this, Father would shoot prairie chickens. Father knew where they roosted at night so he dug a large hold nearby and before daylight he would crawl into this den with his gun and when the birds began their humming he would often shoot several. The old musket came in handy many times. Father made a boat and fish net and our neighbors would join him on fishing trips. Then they would bring home the wagonbox half-full of fine fish: pickerel, perch, suckers, buffalo and bullheads. Much of this we would salt and dry. We didn't raise many chickens but I remember our first setting hen. She set on eleven eggs and hatched eleven fine chickens. A perfect record, wasn't it?

Christmas was a memorable time with us. It began with a festival meal on Christmas Eve of browned spare ribs, potatoes, bread, butter, cheese, rice soup and coffee. When the supper work was done up and we children were bathed and dressed up in our new things, Mother always tried to have something new for us each Christmas. Father would read the Christmas gospel and together we would sing Christmas songs. Father and Mother had good voices and they made good use of them. Christmas morning mother rose early to get the house warm. She always left a little light burning all night, a little kerosene lamp. I still have the habit of leaving a little light on at night because my Mother did it.

Father had early morning devotion and after the morning chores were done, Father would read the Christmas text from Lars Lindrot's *Test Book*. That was one of the good books Mother saved from the fire in Wisconsin. And again they would sing Christmas hymns. It wasn't only on Christmas Day that Father read these sermons, it was every Sunday when we didn't have Church. That was a Sunday routine and we chlidren had to sit still through it, too.

We never had a Christmas tree in our home and for many years no presents were exchanged. I remember well the first Christmas gifts our parents gave us, they were small woolen neck scarfs. My brothers' were blue and white and mine was red and white. My brothers never owned a toy but I did have a doll. When the neighbor girls came to play with me, we would play house in the wagon box with my doll.

Back in pioneer days there wasn't much to buy clothing with and what we bought had to be durable. For several years Father made our shoes from the tops of his boots. Mother knit our mittens and stockings from homespun yarn. I still have the spinning wheel Father made for Mother. My everyday dresses were made of denim. For school I had blue and white checked gingham dresses but for Sunday and dress up I had pretty calico dresses and a white bonnet. I got my first straw hat when I was fifteen and I can see it yet. It was tan and had a wide brim with blue ribbons and a few flowers on it.

When I started school I had no winter coat so I wore my Mother's. It was of heavy wool, homespun. She would tie her wedding shawl around my shoulders and with my warm scarf around my head and my fingers tucked into warm mittens, I was ready for school. When brother John got a new overcoat I got his and it fit me too. I didn't have overshoes until I was fifteen.

My Mother was my best teacher. She taught me all the practical things I needed to know. I was quite a small girl when she taught me how to spin, knit and sew by hand and I enjoyed it. Mother taught me how to pray. She taught me how to read and write, and of course we used the Norwegian language at that time. But I believe the most valuable thing my mother taught me was to trust in God. I can't remember of ever seeing my Mother angry; she never complained and took her lot in life with contentment, for she always looked at the bright side of things.

My mother was tall and slender. She had bright blue eyes and dark hair. She wore it parted in the middle and to see if it was parted she would look into a clear dish of water. We had no mirrors then. We had no clocks either, the sun was our clock when it shone, and when it didn't, we guessed and we didn't always have the right time. Mother was never in a hospital nor a movie. She didn't make a name for herself in the world through club activities or Ladies' Aid for there weren't any.

Mother lost her health quite early and then I had to take over the household duties, but Mother was always there to direct me. Our kind neighbor women sometimes would come in and do up a heavy washing. Before I was able to do the heavy pieces Father would rub them, and he kneaded the bread for me too. Mother would tell me when it was ready for the oven and when it was baked. Mother and I were constant companions and I am happy for it.

One of the first things pioneers did, after establishing a home, was to organize a congregation and lay plans for a church. That was certainly true of Norwegian Valley as that community was called. Father helped to organize the Effata Lutheran Church and that was in 1878. For many years our services were held in the Midway schoolhouse which was built about that time. At first we were not financially able to call a pastor but neighboring pastors served us. We had no Sunday School or Bible School so our spiritual training rested on Father and Mother. As a little girl I used to think my father would have made a good minister because he could explain things so well to us. For confirmation we not only memorized the Catechism and Explanation but the Bible History too. And Father always tested us to see if we knew our lessons.

Father was deacon of Effata or Midway congregation for many years. The first couple to be married out in that community was in the fall of 1881. That was the first wedding I attended. The first child born to the pioneer parents in that community was Rhodena Severson.

The first crop raised on our farm was wheat. Father broke the sod with walking plow drawn by a pair of oxen, then he dragged the ground and finally he handseeded it. Father's first seeder was an interesting one. It was the grain sack that had served as his traveling bag when he made his first trip from Wisconsin to Dakota. It was partially filled with grain, folded to remain open and securely strapped to his shoulder. Then with rhythmic step and steady swing of the arm, Father would scatter the seed. We raised mostly wheat, oats and flax; it wasn't until shortly before we left the farm that we turned to raising much corn. Father's first corn planter was a hand planter.

We were fortunate in having good crops most of the time. I remember one year how a strong wind blew the seed oats right out of the ground and some years later a hail storm ruined much of the crop but we never had a complete crop failure. Our first grain Father cut with the cradle and Mother bound it. Our first harvester was an Adams and French platform harvester. It was so large that it took three oxen to pull it and two men to bind the grain. John and I took turns leading the oxen. We had quite a time. They didn't seem to lead so as to pull evenly, the third ox lagged behind. Father thought he could remedy that so he prodded him on with a good lash of the whip. He lunged forward and broke the evener and when Father went to repair it, he found it had been put on wrong. Ox number three had been pulling the whole load.

Threshing was an interesting time in pioneer days. The separator was run by horse power and I remember it took four or five teams of horses to turn it. Someone with a good sense of balance would stand in the center and prod the horses round and round. It took the whole neighborhood to do a run of threshing. As many as six men handled the bundles, two cut the bands, one to feed the separator, one to care for the separator, one measured grain (one-half bushel measures were used), one man held the sack, another tied it, two men hauled the grain, one shoveled it back in the bin and, last but not least, one packed the straw in the stack. It took twenty-one men to complete the operation. It was no joke to cook for threshers back in those days.

Early on the morning of October 12, 1880, Father and brother John started for Flandreau with a few sacks of wheat to be ground into flour. When they were halfways a terrific snowstorm overtook them. (South Dakota's weather was unpredictable then, too, for the evening before the mosquitoes had been buzzing.) Father turned back and the snow was so blinding that he left it to the good sense of the oxen to find the way home. They took a number of short cuts and it wasn't until they dodged the well that Father knew where they were. Mother and I were just having a cup of coffee when they came, we had been more than busy carrying extra hay and water.

Twisted hay was our fuel in those days. The snowfall was very heavy and it took us days to dig out from under it. There was not a building in sight, everything was buried in snow and you would see smoke curling out of the mounds of snow where the neighbor's house was.

We had three different houses when we were on the farm. The first two were sod houses. The second sod house was built near the road which is now Highway 77 and was quite an improvement over the first. It was built over a cellar, had a good roof, floor, and a kitchen built on. The walls were clay-plastered and clay-washed so it was cheerful. We used our same furniture.

In 1887, Father built our frame house; it was a two story, five room house with hallway and closets and a good basement. Our new house was a joy to us in many ways. We had prospered so we could get some new furniture, even a handpowered Maytag washing machine and was I happy! We hung curtains from the windows and had a carpet on the floor in the parlor. The carpet had been woven from rags dyed red and yellow and made a pretty plaid pattern. A thick layer of clean straw served as padding. And best of all, I didn't have to wear denim dresses any more.

The neighbors had a surprise party on Father and Mother and gave them two big rocking chairs, one for each of them. Our farm buildings were stables at first built of field stone; they served as foundations for a frame structure built later. In 1900 Father built a 30x60x15 foot barn equipped with rope tackles, hay fork and slings.

To keep a good water supply was quite a problem at first. Pioneers used to witch for water. They would take a v-shaped willow branch, hold each end firmly, then walk around the yard and when they passed over a water vein the branch would turn towards the ground. Many of Father's friends did that for him but Father didn't get a chance to develop any faith in water witching for it didn't seem to work. Father had eight wells inside of eleven years. Most of them were shallow wells; three were dug at 100 feet but lasted only a few years. In 1891, Father hired a professional well driller; he struck a good water vein at 247 feet. The supply is still good. The water was too hard for cooking so Father dug a brick-filtered cistern near the house for rain water.

After we got our good well we were able to raise more cattle, sheep, and hogs. I even tried my hand at turkeys. I sold fifty-four of them at nine cents a pound. I got $27.00 for them. I was only sixteen at that time and I thought it was a lot of money for a pioneer girl to call her own. Farm products didn't bring you much in those days. Hogs were four cents a pound, eggs were six cents a dozen, and butter fresh from the churn was five cents a pound. But we could buy a few bargains too. Coffee was seven pounds for a dollar, and calico could be had for three cents a yard. Father put up a windmill and bought a feed grinder and ground feed on shares. That brought us added income.

We were fortunate not to have many bad accidents on the farm. When Fred was six years old he was run over by a bundle wagon. It was my job to lead the oxen for Father and Fred would stand on the tongue and brush the flies off the backs of the oxen. When I was told to lead, Fred would step back to the rack ladder but this time he slipped and in trying to crawl out, the wheel ran over his stomach. We were an anxious family for many days but Fred came out all right.

We children didn't have many toys but our pets were very dear to us. Pat was our first dog and such a pal, many an hour did we play with him. Our first cat was black and was named Mons. We didn't have any riding horses so we rode the calves and the pigs.

My brother John wanted to be a school teacher so after finishing the public school he went to the Agricultural College at Brookings and later to the Normal at Madison where he got a certificate. He had taught a number of years when his health began to fail and after three years of sickness he died, a victim of consumption. I can remember how brave Mother was. John died about noon and that same evening

Mother was able to read her Bible and sing praises. John and I had been very close and many a task we had done together. The last thing John said to Fred was, "Be good to Anna" and Fred surely lived up to it. John was the first adult to be buried in Midway Cemetery.

The fall after John's death I had my first vacation. Lucy Ellingson and I spent Christmas and the New Year holidays with her sister at Cedar Rapids, Iowa. I'll never forget that New Year's Eve. It marked the turn of the century and every bell and whistle in town proclaimed it. The Twentieth Century was ushered in. That was the only Christmas I spent away from my folks.

Father and Mother started out with 160 acres of land, that was in 1878. In the early '80's, Father added forty acres by buying a portion of the school section that joined our land. In 1891, Father bought another quarter of land. He paid $1100.00 for it and by 1897 it was all paid for.

Father was a hard worker and a good manager. But hard work and long hours were beginning to show on both Father and Mother; they were tired so they began thinking about retiring. In many families the farm work was taken over by the sons but not in our family. Brother John was dead and brother Fred was not destined to be a farmer. He wanted an education, he wanted to be a lawyer, so after finishing the public school and high school, he attended Eastern Normal and then Fremont College in Fremont, Nebraska, where he got his Bachelor of Science degree in 1900. He got his degree in law from the University of Nebraska at Lincoln in 1903. The same year he began practicing law in Flandreau.

Father decided to sell the last quarter of land he had bought and move to town in 1901. He built a comfortable two story home there and in 1903 Father and Mother left the farm. Pioneer days were over, the joys and struggles became memories, but the old homestead is still in the Warren family; Clara and I own it.

We children had been brought up in a Christian home and now that time came for us to leave and establish our own homes. We took these Christian principles with us, Fred into his home and I into mine.

Father remained active and was interested in life, especially in church. He was the first one of the pioneers from Norwegian Valley to buy a car. It was a small run-about, a Maxwell. It had no top, no windshield and no clutch, but Father enjoyed driving it.

Mother passed away when she was a little more than eighty-seven years old and a few weeks before her death Father and Mother had celebrated their forty-ninth wedding anniversary. Father continued to live in his home until he passed away at the age of eighty-eight.

Brother Fred died suddenly at his home in Pierre on a Sunday in 1944. He had just come from Church and was reading letters from his children; it was Father's Day when a heart attack took him. Now that Fred was gone I was the only one left of the Warren family and I felt it. But the trust that Mother had taught me came to my help and I knew that since the Lord had chosen me to be the last one to survive, he would care for me. "The Lord is my Shepherd, I shall not want." And I close this family story with the words my mother so often quoted, "The Lord hath given; and the Lord hath taken. The Lord's name be praised."

by Anna Warren Peart, the only surviving member of the family, in 1950

## Kristina Eidsness Tollefson
## Lincoln County
## 1888

Kristina was the third child to be born to Lars and Barbro Eidsness in 1864 in Ekongervaag, Bergen, Norway. The ancestry has been traced back to the year of 1000. Her grandfather served in the Napoleon Wars. Kristina's formal education was limited to reading, figures and writing. Her education in religion, history, folklore and hard work was an endowment from generations who had survived, prospered, and made their country a democracy.

At seventeen Kristina was a capable seamstress. From early spring until the holidays she visited the many fjord homes where she did their annual sewing. The fifth Christmas a change came into her life from across the sea.

A neighbor boy who had immigrated to the United States at the age of seventeen returned as a citizen and landowner looking for a wife. A short courtship, a wedding, and they set sail for America. They were given second class accommodations because ten immigrants were in their party.

It was John's bonus for securing new settlers for the prairies of the West. It was Easter Sunday, 1888 when the party of thirteen arrived in Canton. The residue of the blizzard of '88 covered the land. John secured a spring wagon and horses while the others ate a hasty dinner at the Thompson House.

"The little town was soon left behind us and we were out on the open prairie, deep mud, smokeless shacks and dead animals."

The day was ending when the sun's last rays reflected on the little gray house in whose shadow Uncle Ole Rommereim and good wife Ragnhild were waiting. The heritage Kristina had left in Norway she again found on the Dakota prairies. There was no shack too small or no cupboard too bare for kinfolk or stranger on the way to a better life.

The first week in Norway township Kristina learned of the hazards of weather which brought fear of life, delinquent payments and taxes, the art of baking bread and moving into her new home. The clock ticked, the borrowed stove needed fuel, their trunk was on the table. Uncle Ole gave them three hens and a rooster. Lotta Hanson from across the road to the north brought a cluck hen and a dozen eggs. Old Severt from the local post office brought a gallon of molasses. Signe Sand came with chatter.

Their first son Tollef was born in December. Rebecca, a kind neighbor, was the midwife.

No one escaped the hardships of pioneer life, be it homesteaders or settlers, their future was dependent on their interests in neighbors, church, school, government and family.

Kristina and her husband's home was a haven to many a newcomer whether a stranger or kinfolk. Here they received shelter, food, and faith in a new country. Over the years, many found their way back to feel the warmth of this home. From 1888 to 1930 the Tollefson's lived on their Norway township farm where their community work had radiated far beyond that first prairie shack. They sent forth nine children steeped in culture which has made United States great.

## Ingeborg E. Wangen Buene
## Brown County
## 1883

Ingeborg was born in 1864 in the village of Aurlandsvangen, Sogen, Norway. The village is located down the southwest coast of Norway. It is a lovely place, surrounded by high mountains and beautiful fjords. It was an area noted for its resorts. Life there was like a summer holiday, with the climate neither too hot nor too cold. It attracted tourists the year around. Everyone knew how to sail a boat, ski and skate.

Her parents were Eric Wangen and Ingeborg Anderson. Their family consisted of seven children. Her father was a land owner and also a skilled metal worker (smed in Norwegian). In his youth he trained for this work and was cited for having made a perfect anchor. In villages located on the fjords where boats were indispensable, anchor making was important.

Ingeborg attended the schools available at that time. They were connected with the church, and the headmaster (the presten) was the village clergyman. Reading, writing and arithmetic were greatly stressed, as well as religion and choir music. Ingeborg sang in the church choir and had a fine soprano voice. She was also taught handiwork such as knitting, spinning, sewing and embroidery. These skills were a great asset for any girl to know since all clothing was handmade. Everyone had his own national costume to be used on holidays, and this included special jewelry to be worn with it, such as the Solja.

When Ingeborg came to America, she brought with her a wooden bridal chest. On it were handpainted flowers representing her locality and in it were her most prized possessions. She was nineteen years old when she left Norway and made a nine day voyage across the Atlantic with her brother Christian and a girl friend. They landed in New York City in the spring of 1883 and from there they took a train to Ellendale, Minnesota where sister Anna was already living. From there she went to visit her sister Brita who was already living in Dakota Territory.

In the fall of 1883, she married John Jensen Buene who two years previously (1881) had come to Dakota Territory and "proved up" on a homestead which was located twenty miles north of Aberdeen and only two miles from her sister Brita.

John J. Buene had come to America several years earlier from his family home in Lekangar, Froenningen, Norway. He had come by sailboat and landed in Quebec, Canada in 1869. From there he came directly to Cannon Falls, Minnesota where friends and relatives had located earlier. Then he later came to Dakota Territory, coming to Aberdeen which was known to the early settlers as Sod Town because of the many sod houses.

The surrounding area was just a vast prairie, crisscrossed with buffalo and antelope trails. One of these trails led directly across to a spring which was located on the homestead. Another interesting spot adjoining the homestead was an old Indian Mound. As the pioneers cultivated the soil, many Indian relics and bones were uncovered.

The parents of Ingeborg came to America later and made their home with her family until their deaths.

Her brother, Christian, remained a bachelor and lived on a homestead nearby. In their letters back to Norway describing their life here and severe climate and the early Dakota blizzards, they wrote "We live like the prairie gophers, absorbing sunshine and storing up food in the summer and then hibernating and waiting for the spring thaw."

As the community grew into twelve families who came from Norway as young people, they found they had much in common. A church was organized and built. It was named Aurland Lutheran Church after the village Aurland in Norway. Ingeborg was president of the Ladies Aid for many years and her brother Christian was church secretary for twenty-five years. She had an outstanding soprano voice and her nieces and nephews often remarked, "No matter how large the congregation, we can always hear Aunt Ingeborg's voice."

Outside of caring for her own home and being an active church member, she was called upon very often to help some neighbor through some illness. It was a common occurrence for her children to wake up in the morning to find that she had been called away in the night to help deliver a child or care for some sick neighbor.

As the time went on, her five daughters were all baptized and confirmed in the little country church. Regular church attendance was always emphasized.

Every Christmas there was the traditional Christmas program with every child participating. The huge tree was at the front of the church before the altar and was lighted with a hundred candles. Two of the young men of the congregation always acted as candle snuffers. They stood in constant attention to watch for fire. Their position was always the envy of the younger children. One humorous incident in connection with rehearsals for these programs was the advice given by the (klokar) who trained the children. He said, "Never look at the audience when you are speaking your piece, always keep your eye on the nail above the back door of the church." In spite of his eccentric methods, the programs were good training.

It was also traditional every Christmas for each of the five daughters to have a new dress.

The ride to and from the church was always a thrill. Everyone was huddled into bobsleds which were complete with horses, sleighbells, fur robes, foot warmers, furlined coats and hoods. The ride home at midnight in the snow which sparkled like a million diamonds and the sound of the horses' hooves on the crisp, cold snow, was an experience to be remembered all one's life.

Between Christmas and New Years, this community observed the old Norwegian custom of "Jule boken". The young people, dressed in costume and masked, went in groups from house to house playing what musical instruments they might have and singing carols. They sang until they were invited in to lunch.

The church served as the community center in pioneer days and the church spires on the prairie were like beacons for the early settlers.

One of the tragedies in Ingeborg's life was the loss of photographs, family relics and jewelry when her sister Brita's house burned. She lived with her sister for a short time before her marriage. Incidentally, when these two sisters were seen together, so the letters say, people would remark "What (vakker) women and what beautiful complexions these newcomers have!"

## Margret Hjelmeland Knutson
## Aurora County
## 1882

In the year 1861, my parents and two young sons, four and two years of age, left Bergen, Norway and sailed for the United States. They were nine weeks crossing the ocean.

There was much sickness and many deaths on board. On reaching midocean, the four year old son died and was lowered into the ocean with many others who had died. On nearing land, the two year old son died. They were allowed to hold his body until they reached Quebec, where he was laid away.

They settled on a rented farm near Morris, Illinois, where they lived a number of years. Nine more children were added to the family; two more children died while living there. I (Martha) was the youngest of eleven children. When I was two and one-half months old, my father died, leaving Mother destitute with seven children. After Father's death, Mother moved to Rowe, Illinois.

In 1880 and 1881, rumors of the wonderful climate, soil and opportunities for homemaking reached Pontiac and Rowe, Illinois. Many families prepared to venture into the wilderness to make their fortune and face the Indians and coyotes.

Margaret Knutson, a widow with seven children, had two reasons for wishing to come to Dakota Territory. First reason was that her daughter Anna, thirteen years old, had tuberculosis of the lungs. She had been told the climate in the territory was wonderful in healing lung trouble. (Thanks to the climate and Dr. Brown of Plankinton, Anna lived to be the mother of ten children and died at the age of eighty-two years.)

Her second reason was to establish a home for her children. Mrs. Knutson decided to wait until some of her friends and neighbors had become established who would then be in a position to advise her whether or not it might be a good move.

Their Pastor at Rowe, Rev. Ole Tjomsland and family, with Mrs. Knutson's eldest daughter Isabell, had departed for Dakota Territory the previous year. Mrs. Knutson came west with a couple of neighbors the following year in the fall. All were so favorably impressed with the country that they all took claims. Mrs. Knutson's claim is located in Aurora County. On her return to Illinois, Mrs. Knutson borrowed $200.00 and after a couple months, she with her two youngest children and old friends chartered a car for the new country, their destination being Mitchell. They were met by Isabell, Rev. Tjomsland and Barney Helgerson, an old friend from Rowe, Illinois. Mrs. Knutson inquired where the town was located? Mr. Helgerson informed her THIS was Mitchell.

They all bundled themselves up with quilts over their heads, in their wagon, and continued on their journey to the home of Rev. Tjomsland located eighteen miles northwest of Mitchell. Their home was very small, with an attic upstairs. When Mrs. Knutson arrived there were already three families there. Nevertheless, room was made for all. The children were obliged to perch on the ladder to the attic most of the time in order to give the elders the small floor space.

When night came they wondered how sleeping quarters could be arranged, as the Tjomsland family occupied the only two beds. This was soon settled, the men began carrying armfuls of hay and scattered it over the floor. At bedtime each family gathered their brood into separate corners and made their beds. The elders did much laughing and joking about leaving their comfortable homes and feather beds to come to Dakota Territory to sleep on the floor and burn twisted hay.

Mrs. Knutson stayed at the Tjomsland home about three weeks before her shanty was completed, retarded by stormy weather. Then she journeyed to her claim, eight miles northwest of Mt. Vernon. Tying her two cows she'd brought with her from Illinois behind the wagon, and quilts over their heads, they started on their way, stopping on the way where two Russian bachelors lived to purchase a couple loads of hay, one load which was to be delivered that night. (This was March 4, 1882.)

Her shanty was 12X14, built from twelve inch boards which had shrunk considerably, leaving wide tracks in the roof and walls, the roof having no shingles but the twelve inch boards. No door was made to be hung, nor any windows cut out.

After a couple days a blizzard set in from the northwest. Quilts were nailed from the peak of the ceiling to the floor. Mrs. Knutson had taken the door from an upstairs closet on leaving her home in Illinois which came into fine use at this time.

Fearing her two cows, who were picketed at the haycock, would suffer, she tied quilts around each cow with ropes and brought the chicken crate with a dozen chickens into the shack. The lamp was lit day and night since there was no window. She feared the fire would go out at night as twisted hay did not burn long. She had purchased a half-ton of coal, which was piled on the ground and which was used sparingly at night.

She walked nine miles to Tjomsland's for her first pound of butter, later walking the same distance to Plankinton for her next pound of butter and a box of matches, as her cash was rather low.

Our nearest neighbor, Daniel Webster, put in our first window in May, a twenty-four inch four-pane window, a treat never to be forgotten by the children. Later Mr. and Mrs. Ole Kirkus and three children came from Rowe, Illinois, staying at Mrs. Knutson's until their shanty was built. James Jacobson, John Tolleen and Thorwald Myers, all bachelors, also stayed there while completing their claim shanties.

Again there was not enough room for the children. This time they were kept in bed where they had to remain all day, passing the time playing with their dolls. Having no room for a table, a flat top chest was used, the dishes placed in a box in a corner and covered.

In the spring, Mr. Myers and Mr. Tolleen dug a basement under the three-foot walls of the shanty, making another extra room, which was a joyful addition to the former skimpy quarters.

Mr. Jacobson broke the first ten acres for oats and a half-acre for garden. All the garden sod was cut into two-foot strips and Mrs. Knutson carried every foot of it to sod up the three-foot sides and ends of her shanty. At this time they enjoyed the comforts of the extra room, which was to them their first floor.

A picket fence of sticks and laths placed far enough apart to keep out chickens was soon constructed in pioneer style around the little garden. Mrs. Knutson's three other children arrived from Illinois in August and her oldest son, later. After their arrival, Mrs. Knutson went to Mitchell to cook at the Bradley House which became a popular rendezvous for the influx of pioneers in the early eighties. In this way she earned enough money to buy a team of oxen with which to break up the virgin soil, and also which put an end to her eight and nine mile walks to Mt. Vernon or Plankinton to purchase groceries.

On a very warm day when Mrs. Knutson's grocery supply was low, she, with Mrs. Kirkus, dressed in their best Sunday apparel (becoming in those days) and yoked up the oxen for a journey to Mt. Vernon. On the way they had to pass a large slough. The oxen, determined to cool off, waded out into the middle, stopped contentedly, drinking and swishing their tails to drive off the mosquitoes and flies, when the tongue dropped out of the yoke.

Mrs. Knutson, thinking she might walk out on the tongue and by hanging onto the yoke, might reach down and replace the tongue. But her feet slipped and she plunged full length into the water. The trip was long remembered by both women.

The first school in that community was taught by Miss Minnie Cook in her claim shanty two miles west, with twelve pupils. She later became the wife of Dr. R. F. Brown. The pupils played many pranks on the teacher when he drove out as school closed, to take her for a ride with his dashing black steeds.

On January 12, 1888, was the day of the great blizzard. On this particular morning the sky was overcast but still and balmy, growing colder at noon. At twelve o'clock the blizzard struck with all its fury. The teacher forbade any of the pupils to leave for their homes. About four o'clock two young men arrived with a market basket filled to scripture measure, which Mrs. Knutson had prepared and sent by her oldest son Knute, and a friend, who arrived safely to everyone's joy and surprise, and who also remained there for the night. Many people and much livestock froze to death during the blizzard.

Mrs. Knutson always said the happiest days of her life were spent in South Dakota. She passed away at the age of seventy years and was buried in the cemetery on her old homestead which she still owned at the time of her death.

by Martha Knutson Allen, her youngest child

# Kristianna Ortness Trygstad
# Brookings County
# 1869

Kristianna was born in 1816 in Vardalen, Norway, and married Nils Trygstad in 1838. He was a caretaker or worker on the Trygstad farm in Vardalen, a tailor, and sewed clothes for the family who owned the farm. He received very little pay, so the family lived in great poverty. Often the children had to go to bed hungry, and they had very few clothes. Their food consisted mainly of bread made from a coarse oat flour and some barley flour, potatoes and herring.

Nils and Kristianna had nine children, two of which passed away in infancy. As soon as they were able, their seven sons had to go out to work to help make a living. The work that they did was mainly herding cattle and sheep. The Lutheran church that the family belonged to was called Stiklestad, and filled a very important place in their lives. Their pastor's name was "Prosten Kok." He confirmed all the children except the two youngest, who were confirmed in America.

Life was difficult for them because of their small earnings and since there seemed no hope of anything better in the future if they remained in Norway, they decided to emigrate to America, leaving the first part of May, 1866. They went from Vardalen to Throndhjem where they stayed a week while the ship was loaded. The name of the ship was "Victor," a sailing ship.

After traveling six weeks across the Atlantic, they finally landed in Quebec the middle of June. They stayed there for a few days so they had a chance to do a little sightseeing. They traveled on the railroad from Quebec to Detroit, Michigan. From there they took a boat across Lake Michigan to Milwaukee and a train to La Crosse. From there they went by boat on the Mississippi to Winona where they transferred to a train to complete their journey to Rochester, Minnesota.

A railroad bridge had burned west of Winona, so the passengers had to walk some distance to another train which took them to Rochester. The train coaches in which they traveled were box cars with benches along the sides. These box cars were not very clean or pleasant to ride in as they had been used for stock before they were converted to passenger use.

That summer the family stayed at the home of Nils Lokve, where their brother Ole, who had come to America the year before, worked. After that the family lived in Salem, Minnesota, near Rochester, for three years.

In May, 1869, two of Kristianna and Nils' sons, Martin and Erik, started out on foot from their home near Rochester to go to the unknown west in search of free government land where they might establish a home. During that gloomy, rainy day they managed to get a little way beyond Blooming Prairie. They slept out under some bushes that night and the second day they reached Waseca. The third day they went to St. Peter, Minnesota. Here they went to the land office and inquired about available land. They were told to go to Yellow Medicine County as there was much good land there.

It took them two days to get to Fort Ridgly which they passed and went on to Redwood Falls where they were told to follow the south side of the Redwood River to Lynd, Minnesota, where there was free land and timber. They reached Lynd by evening and stayed there overnight. The next day they were heading for Lake Benton, the last white settlement, but got on a wrong road and passed it. They continued west and reached the Sioux River about three miles north of Medary. They had no food so they tried to fish but did not get any. They stayed there overnight and the next morning started back to Lake Benton, Minnesota. It took them three days to go from Lynd to Sioux River and back to Lake Benton. They left Lake Benton for Redwood Falls and met their family with the immigrant load between Redwood Falls and New Ulm.

The group went west to the Big Sioux River about four miles southwest of what is now the city of Brookings, and four miles northwest of the place that soon became the early settlement or town of Medary. (This town site was later abandoned and the town of Brookings grew up.) Here on the east bank of the river they decided to settle, as the land near the river was fertile, and there was abundance of grass and running water for the stock and also plenty of timber from which they could build their home. Thus originated the first permanent white settlement in Brookings County, South Dakota.

An attempt was made at a settlement here earlier. An expedition representing the "Dakota Land Company" of St. Paul, traveling with ox teams from New Ulm, reached Dakota Territory in the summer of 1857, located a townsite near the Big Sioux River in the southern part of the county and named it Medary, in honor of the governor of Minnesota. It was their plan that this should become the capital of the new territory.

Major DeWitt with a group of about fourteen men built quarters and remained through the following winter, but in the spring of 1858 a hostile group of Sioux Indians ordered them away. The whites obeyed and there was no bloodshed. The settlers already had planted some potatoes but the Indian squaws [sic] dug up the seed and prepared a feast. Later, after a permanent settlement was established on the same site, settlers discovered relics including household utensils and farm implements that had been thrown into a well and never recovered by the original inhabitants. It was eleven years after Major DeWitt and his men left Medary before the Trygstads came to make a permanent settlement on that site.

The Brookings *County Press* of March 6, 1879, tells of the earliest and biggest scare the Trygstad party had after their arrival in the Medary vicinity in the summer of 1869.

"A short distance from them was seen a large party of Indians passing over a rise of land with ponies with long poles attached, loaded with baggage, squaws, papooses and savage-looking warriors. Their fear was increased by seeing a party of the warriors approaching them. Some of the men caught up their guns and advanced to meet the approaching foe. Slowly and cautiously they approached each other, while the women and children remained huddled together waiting in breathless anxiety the result of the attack. The joy of the party can be better imagined than described, when the approaching savages, instead of rushing them with tom-a-hawks, merely asked for tobacco. The men relaxed their grip upon their guns and gave their visitors a hearty welcome. The Indians were invited to the camp, supplied with the longed for tobacco and, after a short conversation carried on by signs and motions, the new acquaintances parted the best of friends."

As soon as the Trygstad party arrived they built a log house. Their principal wealth consisted of twenty head of cattle and four yoke of oxen, with wagons, farm tools and household furniture. Four houses were built along the river, and the whole party wintered there in 1869-70, thus forming the first permanent settlement in this county, for the residence of some of the brothers or their children has been continuous in that vicinity since. Finding that their first loads of provisions were likely to be inadequate for winter on account of so many Indians demanding food, Martin and Cornelius made a trip to Redwood Falls to the mill in December. On their return home a snow storm, which turned into a blizzard, overtook them. They stopped all night on the prairie near the big slough west of the present site of Elkton. The storm abated and they reached home the following evening, but they had to leave their wagon in a slough within forty rods of the house.

At this time their nearest neighbors were at Flandreau (Jim Jones and some half-breed Indians), their nearest mill at New Ulm, and their post office was Sioux Falls. There was plenty of snow during the winter, but timber was a good protection and they passed the winter in "reasonable" comfort. Until 1879 no case of serious sickness occurred. After that date medical men were plentiful.

Kristianna was very lonely that first winter in the new unknown West. She was far from her own family and friends, and did not even have any other women friends close enough so that she could see them or visit with them over a cup of coffee. Then, too, there were no conveniences at all, and everything had to be done the hard way. Kristianna was used to hard work, but this was even harder than she'd been used to. Pioneering was especially hard for women, but they proved themselves able to "take it" and to come through it as well as the men.

In January, 1871, M. N. Trygstad and two other men were appointed commissioners to organize the county. Governor John A. Burbank at the same time appointed a register of deeds and located the county seat at Medary.

The Martin Trygstad home was for a time the county seat and was at all times the central place for the meetings held by the settlers to advise over public matters. Martin Trygstad was the first county superintendent of schools, and in 1872 was elected the first member of the territorial legislature and was later a senator from Brookings County.

In 1873, the Pay brothers from Oakwood accompanied by Martin Trygstad and two other Medary men, served as the first jurors from Brookings County before a court at Pembina, now in North Dakota. They made the journey in a wagon drawn by mules. On their trip, they reported seeing no settlers between Oakwood and Fargo, North Dakota.

At this time there was no minister among the settlers so they would gather in the homes on Sundays and conduct their own services. They would read Scripture and one of Martin Luther's sermons from a book of sermons which they had brought with them. Their faith was very dear to them as was shown by the fact that they brought their devotional books, hymn books, catechisms, and Bibles with them from Norway, and used them regularly.

The Trygstads were very helpful to the newcomers. They gave freely of time and money to the newcomers and helped them select good pieces of land. When it was necessary they would help them in other and more material ways to get a start in the new country.

The first school ever held in Brookings County was at Medary in the winter of 1874 and 1875. Mr. Gulbertson, then only a youth, taught school. He was not qualified for it but the parents wanted a teacher and he and young Henry Stearns were the only eligible young men in the community, and Henry wouldn't "tackle it." Neither of them had completed the eighth grade and felt somewhat timid about trying to teach others. However, Mr. Gulbertson finally agreed, provided Mr. Stearns would help him. The school room was 12x14. The teacher's desk was a dry goods box and was the only desk in the room. The seats were one kitchen chair for the teacher and for the pupils, three benches made of ten foot boards with peg legs at the ends for supports.

Growth of the little village of Medary, four miles from the Trygstad settlement, is indicated by a newspaper item of 1876 which reads:

"The place has grown from a few unpainted buildings apparently used for dwellings, to a genuine village. The extensive planting of ornamental and shade trees, together with the erection of the hitching posts and horse blocks, lead an individual to mentally exclaim, 'These people are hopeful for the future and expect to live in full'."

By 1879 the village of Medary had become quite a trade center and several lines of business were represented. However, the railroad came through Brookings in November, 1879, and most of the buildings were moved from Medary to Brookings.

As this went on, Kristianna Trygstad saw her children marry and have children and establish their own homes and become good citizens in the community. She saw many changes and improvements in their own farm and home as well as in the nearby town and the community round about. She came to love dearly this adopted land of hers, and felt that it was truly home.

She died in 1900, and was buried in a little cemetery a few miles from their home, and close to Lake Campbell.

by Marie Trygstad Graves

# THE SWEDES

## Hilma Rudine Olson
## Hyde County
## 1883

Hilma Rudine was born in Morlunda, in the south central part of Sweden on March 31, 1872 to Mr. and Mrs. Gustaph Adelph Johnson who later changed their last name to Rudine after they came to America. Hilma's father came to America in 1883. After trying several other places, he came to Highmore. As it hadn't achieved statehood yet it was known as Dakota Territory and he filed on a homestead twenty miles north of Highmore in what is now Illinois township.

Mr. Rudine built a sod house and sent for his family. In 1885 Hilma, along with her mother, sister and brothers, came from Sweden to Highmore and to the sod house her father had ready for them. They lived in it for about a year and then it burned down and they moved into the granary. Later on Hilma's father bought a house and had it moved on the place.

Heating homes in the pioneer days was a major problem, especially in the vicinity where Hilma lived with her parents, as there wasn't a tree in sight. One of the unique ways they had of heating was a straw burner. They used a big tub in oblong shape and packed it as tightly as possible with straw. Lids were removed from the cook stove and the tub of straw turned upside-down over the stove. The flames would slowly start to burn the straw, then increase until it was burning like fury. The house ranged from being downright cold to extreme heat.

Although Hilma was reluctant to leave home she knew the family needed financial assistance and went to work as a seamstress in the Loui Ramsey Tailor Shop in Pierre. The building was also occupied by the Heglunds Music Store. Hilma did some sewing for Scotty Phillips while working there. The cowboys all carried guns and when they came to Pierre everyone would get off the streets and let them take over the town.

In January, 1897, while Hilma was still employed at the Tailor Shop, her brother, Carl Oscar, passed away at the age of twenty-one. It was a winter with a heavy snow cover, at least four feet on the level. Can you imagine the hardship that would cause along with all the heartache of losing a loved one? All of the neighbors stood by and did whatever they possibly could do.

Hilma was married December 24, 1898 to Charles F. Olson, a widower with one child, a boy eight years old named Emil. The ceremony was held at the bride's home in Illinois township and was performed by Rev. Thurstore. All the neighborhood attended and Hilma's mother, with the help of Hilma and her sister August, prepared all the food. After the ceremony the couple moved to a farm in Spring Lake township. There all five of their children were born at home.

An addition was built to the house to accommodate a growing family and then they were plagued with water problems and finally decided they would have to move. They bought land a half-mile from where they were located. They bought the land from Mr. Habe who was selling out after the tragic loss of his wife. Mr. Habe and his wife were on their way to the barn in a blizzard to do chores. They were holding hands for protection but the wind tore them apart and Mrs. Habe became lost in the blizzard. Her frozen body was found just a few rods from the barn several days later.

Then began the tremendous job of moving to their new location. Bart Mitchell was the owner of the moving rig and this is the way the moving of the four-room house was accomplished.

The house was jacked up and planks were fastened to the bottom of it. The planks were laid on the ground lengthwise under the house extending ahead of it. Steel rollers were slid under the house crosswise between the planks. One end of a long cable was fastened to the planks on the house. The other end was fastened to a winch. A horse was hitched to a drive wheel and went around and around in a circle, turning the winch and wrapping the cable around it, slowly drawing the house forward. Then the men would pick planks and rollers, carry to the front of the house, move the winch and drive wheel ahead and the same procedure would be continued.

It took six days to move the house a half mile and the amazing thing is that the family lived in the house all during the moving. Meals were cooked, baking was done, dishes were washed and all the rest of the household duties went on as usual. Emma Brick worked for Hilma and helped out during the moving. After the house was moved another addition was built on.

Earning a living was no small job to the pioneer farmer and his wife. At one time Charles and Hilma milked twenty cows. Hilma would set the milk to cool in shallow pans then when the cream came to the top she would skim it off with a spoon and churn it to butter in a barrel-type churn. It would be packed into twenty-five pound butter tubs and hauled by team and wagon twenty-seven miles to Highmore where it would be shipped by train to Chicago. The price they received was twelve cents a pound. The neighbors took turns hauling the butter to town. After the butter business failed they switched to selling sour cream.

Charles raised thoroughbred horses, such as Percherons, Belgians and Clydesdales. This required him to be away from home quite often. Besides that, he served as county commissioner for several years beginning in 1907 and he would have to stay in town during the meetings which sometimes lasted two weeks. At these times all the responsibilities of the farm rested on Hilma, along with all her other duties.

She made all of the family clothing. Calico was the popular type of cloth then. She had a lot of cooking to do. Food was bought in large quantities in the fall to last all winter: syrup, flour, sugar, crackers and dried fruit consisting of peaches, prunes, apples and apricots. She would send to a fish company in Northern Minnesota for a fifty pound drum of lutefisk. It had to be soaked in a lye water solution before it could be eaten. Hens didn't lay eggs in the winter as in the fall. Hilma would mix a chemical with water in a twenty gallon crock and that would make a jelly-like solution. Hilma would put the eggs in that and they would keep all winter.

At butchering time Hilma would pack the pork in twenty gallon crocks in a salt water solution. Another method was to dig a pit and from the pit a trench, a few feet long. A stove pipe would be laid in the trench and a barrel with the bottom taken out was put over the end of the stove pipe. The meat was hung in the barrel and holes punched in the lid. The pit was filled with wood from ash trees and old wagon wheel spokes which were made of hickory. That was set afire and when the fire was burning good the pit was covered and the smoke would go through the stove pipe and up into the barrel. Smoked meat was kept in oatbins in the summer to keep from spoiling.

Hilma raised a large flock of ducks. They not only provided meat but Hilma used the down to make pillows. Charles always had to have his little joke about the ducks. He said they had scoop shovels instead of bills because they ate so much.

Hilma's wash days were a far cry from our present push-button wash days. First of all the house set on top of the hill and the well was at the bottom. Water for washing and the chickens was hauled in barrels on a stone boat pulled up the hill with a team of horses. Hilma's first washing machine was a wooden tub on legs with a handle that you pushed back and forth to run the machine. It was considered a sheer luxury item and it was the children's job to push the handle back and forth, but for some reason they were always hard to find on wash days.

Along with the many other tasks the pioneer wife and mother had to do was doctoring and nursing. Hilma took care of her husband and stepson, Emil, through several bouts of pneumonia. In one case when Charles had pneumonia in the winter the window was kept wide open and a frame with a cloth tacked to it was put in the window to keep the direct draft off from him. Hilma nursed him day and night and had to wear a coat to keep warm while she watched over him.

When any of the children would step on rusty nails or such things, Hilma would make a poultice of oats in a small bag, boil it in water and put it on the wound while still hot. For chest colds she would put oats in a larger bag and heat it in the oven. Then it would be laid on the chest. By 1908 telephones were installed and a doctor could be called and would make the twenty-seven mile trip from Highmore to Charles and Hilma's farm by horse and buggy.

In 1918 a red cross unit was organized and almost the whole neighborhood joined, including Hilma. The ladies knitted socks, sweaters, leggings and wristlets for the soldiers.

In 1917 Charles and Hilma got their first car. They traded a team of horses to Welcome McLaughlin for a car called the Overland.

Beginning from the oldest the children were married. At one time all six couples lived within a radius of six miles from home. Outside of some of them spending a short time in other states, they all ended up in Hyde county and settled there.

Their mother enjoyed company and parties. Memories the children have of their parents and their childhood are many: playing flying dutchman and blind man's bluff, ice skating parties and singing to the playing of the organ, the family's pride and joy. Their mother taking them to Chautauquas when they came to Highmore as she wanted a little culture brought into their lives. Going to church and Sunday school with a horse and buggy to the Sedgwick Church. Boarding a school teacher that gave Edith and Esther lessons on the organ. Coming in from ice skating or sliding down hill and warming up by the hard coal heater. Their mother encouraging them to read books. Gray wolves howling at night. Their dad coming home with loads of hay that sometimes had unwanted hitchhikers: the bull snake. One snake that managed to sneak a ride measured eight feet long.

They would get a big laugh when their dad would drive up to the gate in the car and holler "whoa" to stop it. A life time of hollering "whoa" to horses is hard to break.

Their father enjoying reading his Swedish papers, the *Svenska Americana* and the *Chicago Bladet*.

Most of all, they remember a mother who was always there when they needed her.

## Kristina J. Carlson Johnson
## Hyde County
## 1887

As this is being written, March 15, 1954, there is a radio broadcast over WNAX, Yankton, South Dakota, incident to the dedication of the great Fort Randall Dam at Pickstown. The signal was given by President Eisenhower in Washington, D.C. for Governor Sigurd Anderson of South Dakota to press a button starting the first generator of eight which will produce 320,000 kilowatts. It gives us a sense of pride at the great stride in progress and achievement of our great state of South Dakota since those early territorial days and it gives us a feeling of importance that our parents were among the great number of pioneers, who by their courage, perseverance and endured hardships, bravely contributed so much in paving the way for the many great accomplishments and blessings which we enjoy today.

When she was nine years old her father died and she and her mother spent some time visiting in the home of an aunt and uncle. When a couple years later she acquired a stepfather, her aunt and uncle wished to adopt her, having no children of their own. Her mother did not consent to this, but she remained with them throughout her entire girlhood. As her mother lived a long distance away, they visited with each other very seldom. Therefore, she scarcely knew her two half-sisters and one half-brother.

Then a few years later her stepfather died and she visited with her mother a few months. After a few more years her mother again remarried. By this time she loved her aunt and uncle very much and they loved her. Though not legally adopted, she had all the privileges of a daughter. Her uncle, Arvid Arvidson, was a professor of music and church organist and director of music in a large church, as well. Mother loved music and often wistfully spoke of the huge pipe organ in the church and of the inspiring church music. They had a fine home and employed some seven or eight people for the household and other work. They entertained friends a great deal; it was the custom to serve cocktails to the afternoon and evening callers and guests and at all social occasions. This was usually Kristin's part. They maintained a wine cellar which was customary. Stocked with wine, cognac, champagne and ale, the key to this cellar was entrusted to her entirely. She herself never learned to drink and she was often disgusted with some guest who imbibed too freely. Her girlhood days had been rather carefree and happy and she had danced a lot. Then she met a young man, who neither danced nor drank. They fell in love and were married, May 30, 1872. She was twenty-three, he twenty-four. The wedding was in a large church after having been announced a certain length of time according to church rules. The wedding dress was black, a cameo brooch, a prayer book, white kid gloves and a crown, which was furnished to brides by the church. The groom wore a black Prince Albert outfit, the usual black tie and white kid gloves, all hand made. We still have this coat, now eighty-two years old, the stitching is still good.

They went to live at Hellemolle, on a farm, her husband's parental home, where he was born. Two younger sisters lived with them. It was a nice farm with a two-story house and a little barn across the road. Since she married a farmer, her gift from her mother and stepfather was a yoke of two-year-old oxen, which in the "old country" was considered quite a gift. (A grandniece from Sioux City, Iowa, visited there in 1952 and found this house still there. A cousin picked a water lily for her from a pool nearby.)

Soon three children blessed their home, Carl Walfrid, Gunner Alfrid, and Anna Ulricka. In 1882 an epidemic of diphtheria struck them and the surrounding area, and a great many children died. Doctors were few and overworked. Treatment and cure was unknown at that time. Mother and Father together with many other agonized parents watched their little ones die by strangulation without being able to help. All three, ages seven, five, and two and one-half years, died within a week. That spring a little boy was born. He was named Henry Adrian, weighing five pounds, but he grew to be a tall, normal young man. Three years later, Nels August Severin was born.

Plans were then being made to emigrate to America and the decision to start was made when two and one-half years later a daughter, Huldah Sophia, was born. It was a huge job preparing for the long trip. In those days the tailor, dressmaker and shoemaker came to the homes to prepare the entire wardrobe. Mother had been very busy carding wool, spinning and dyeing, knitting, and weaving a great deal for the family, as the clothing had to last for a long time.

They brought with them quite a number of items, such as the spinning wheel, wool cards, sheep shears, two copper kettles, butcher knife, steel dagger, scissors and some kitchenware made of white steel, which was razor sharp, made by a blacksmithing uncle. They also brought a rosewood jewel box and many other articles.

June 30, 1887, Kristin Johnson, her husband, Nels Alfred Johnson, and three small children arrived in Highmore, Hyde County, Dakota Territory. It was the end of a long tiresome journey, having started from Malmo, Kalmarlan, Smoland, Sweden, May 10, 1887. The voyage across the Atlantic had been very stormy. The boat, a large one of the White Cunnard Lines, had rolled and tossed, with forty foot waves sweeping over the decks, causing the passengers to suffer greatly from sea sickness, all except this writer, who was two weeks old at the time. She seemed to grow and thrive in spite of the limited supply of condensed milk available on board ship. The two small boys, Henry, five, and August, two and one-half, enjoyed the great adventure immensely. The baby at the journey's end was eight weeks old, doing well, thank you!

After the usual delay in New York with the customs officials at Ellis Island, clearance was made of identification papers, baggage and other personal possessions incident to the continuation of the remainder of the journey by rail. They traveled through Quebec, Chicago, and across the great Northwest to Highmore, Dakota Territory without difficulty. Here they were met by a Mr. Dan with a mule team and a very rickety lumber wagon, they then continued on for another twenty miles north "as the crow flies," over a rocky wagon trail.

Mother's heart sank and a wave of momentary homesickness swept over her as she looked over an endless stretch of open prairie. No trees, only an occasional small building in the distance could be seen. But it was a beautiful June day, the sky was blue above. As they rode along her spirits rose, for that endless sea of tall, waving prairie grass and little, wild, red geraniums along the trail was beautiful and the song of the birds, especially the meadowlarks, was cheerful. The children slept to the rattle of the wagon and the clank, clank of the tug chains with an occasional bump over a rock.

Father, however, loved this vast expanse at once; he envisioned great possibilities: a beautiful home, large herds, great fields. The prospect of his reunion with his brother, John Bern, and other friends who had immigrated two or three years before, made him jubilant, indeed. With good health and a family, Kristin, now thirty-six, and he, now thirty-seven, with plenty of ambition; life looked very promising. About fifteen miles along the trail, the mules grew warm and tired, so they stopped to rest by a place on the road. It was the home of August Sunding and what a happy visit that was! Rest, lunch and coffee and so much to talk about as they too, had emigrated from Sweden only a few years previously.

Toward evening they continued on about six miles further north to the home of John Bern and family. "Bern" was a name conferred in the Swedish military upon certain soldiers, that being the reason for different surnames of the brothers. Here they enjoyed visiting for some time. The Gustaf Rudines lived one-half mile west and were friends from their native land.

After a short time, arrangements were made for rooms with other old friends, Charles Allm and his sister, Hannah, who lived in a two-story frame house two miles further northwest. Here they stayed while preparations were made for a location for a new home.

This Scandinavian settlement, mostly Swedes, was the center of what is now the Sedgwick community in Illinois Township. Sedgwick was so named in honor of the family who operated the postoffice in connection with a little store; this Mr. Sedgwick was somewhat of a doctor, also. The post office was located one and one-half miles north of the present location of the Sedgwick Church. There were also English,

German, French, Scotch, and Irish people who lived in this vicinity, also a Bohemian settlement to the east.

Many homesteaders had previously performed their obligations to "Uncle Sam", some having sold their land and moved away. All too soon we learned the reason, as we soon encountered drought ridden years, of which we had heard nothing. The little mounds of dirt, formerly sod shanties, a few rocks, broken pieces of glass and china, rusty barrel hoops and pans, a few bleached bones and gone-back sod gave mute evidence of disappointment and discouragement in the early 80's. Prospectors had rushed in on the Chicago Northwestern Railway which then ended at Pierre, because some of them had heard about the discovery of gold in the Black Hills and other great "get rich quick" schemes promoted by certain irresponsible land companies. The majority came for purposes of establishing homes on promises of large acreages offered by the government. During this time there had been a so-called land survey for a railroad from Pierre to Aberdeen; the survey showed that the railroad would pass through south of the Sedgwick post office and eventually a town would be established at Sedgwick. This partly promoted a thickly-settled community.

Father immediately filed claim to three quarters of land all in a row: a homestead, a pre-emption and a tree claim. The location of the quarters were designated by a rock cornerstone; on each there were carved numerals. By careful searching some may still be found. Then with the help of "Uncle Bern" and some friends plans went forward for a sod house, this was the last in this section of the country. A deep cellar was dug by hand, lumber was hauled for the floors, 2 x 4s for the rafters and studdings and boards for the roof, four windows (size 18 x 24 with real glass panes!)

Good sod was broken, wide bladed slough and bunch grass, and was cut in twenty inch lengths, four or five inches thick, twelve inches wide. Then carefully laid and plastered with a claylike mud between each layer, finally plastered inside and whitewashed, even the rafters and boards in the roof. The roof was carefully covered with sod over heavy tar paper almost like shingles. Ours never leaked even in heavy rainfall. It was a two-room, "L" shaped, gable roofed house. The living room boasted three windows, the kitchen, one window and a door. Though small, it was a very comfortable home. Many happy years were spent there. Friends and neighbors visited often. Mother even managed to entertain at Christmas and other holidays and occasions. Later two children were born and baptized here: Albert Engelbert, September, 1889 and Emma Victoria (Frame), February, 1892.

As we were located along a trail directly into Highmore and Seneca, people often stopped to rest their horses or oxen. Mother would hurry and put her copper tea kettle on and make coffee and don her white apron; a spread of white linen cloth was put on the table. Father and Mother looked forward to these visits. Many times they brought news from other places. This trail soon became the regular mail route and still is, with a few changes. A Mr. Leighty carried mail in all kinds of weather everyday by using ponies and a cart. He would have a large heated rock or lighted lantern at his feet in cold weather. The postoffices were: Hawley, Sedgwick, Zeigler, Goudyville and Dunsmore. He would change ponies along the way. We had mail every day.

Our sod house was located sixty rods west from the present Sedgwick Church site. It brings great memories as we children often played on the rock on that particular little knoll. Father had a little smoke house and a potato field in the low place west of it. He also built a little barn, of which one side was a long, high stone wall; also quite a large stone enclosure for hogs and calves. These rocks are still there. Also a rock wall enclosing a garden. Many of these rocks went into the church foundation in 1908. The barn was built with some lumber, a partial sod roof and part hay shed, making a fair barn. A shallow well for water was dug by hand, which furnished water many months depending upon the amount of rain and snow fall. This water was used for washing and for our big white cow and a young ox.

This first cow, called "Bossy", served a dual purpose in furnishing milk and as a draft animal. She helped the ox draw a stone boat and barrel for water hauling and in moving rocks of which we had found we had a large surplus so well hidden by the tall grass. Father spent many back breaking weary hours and days clearing rocks from the fields at which he was surprised and dismayed. Though not rocky land, there were still plenty when it came time to break the sod.

The next year another well about twenty feet deep was dug on a little elevation near a deep slough, which was usually full of snow water every spring. It was equipped with wooden curbing, a wooden bucket and long rope and fixed so that no surface water could seep in. It also had a tight cover. It had a gravel bottom and it furnished delicious cold water for drinking, cooking and all purposes. Sometimes it furnished water until fall or later. What a wonderful blessing that was! Mother was very happy about this. It was cleaned at least once every year, insuring pure, clean water.

During the winter months it was necessary to haul water in barrels on a stone boat from a deep well two miles east. There was great difficulty in keeping the water from freezing solid in the barrels. In zero weather the barrel was rolled inside the kitchen door. Later we were lucky in getting our water from our neighbor, John Jensen, who lived three-fourths miles north. He had been fortunate in securing a good bored well of very good water.

That first winter Father decided to find some work away from home. The only job to be had was on the railroad at Highmore. He found a place to board and room at the home of a Mrs. Major. He walked home Saturday evenings after work, twenty-two miles and back on Sunday night or early Monday morning. Two years later after his crop had dried out he worked a short time in Aberdeen, [perhaps she means a closer town] walking home Saturday nights in order to spend Sunday with his family. Due to the great distance he did not do this too often. A Swedish crown being worth about one-third of an American dollar, many crowns were needed in this country in purchasing the many items needed.

Those were lonesome and worrisome times for Mother with three small children and no telephone in those days, of course. The nearest neighbor, though one-half miles away (an English couple, Mr. and Mrs. Sperling), were very kind and neighborly, but very difficult for Mother to make herself understood. It required the utmost in courage and Christian faith at this time. Mother had a quiet and patient serenity and a great capacity for understanding. She was unafraid and if she was frightened we children never saw any signs of it. She was never hampered by any superstition as she said that that was contrary to the Bible. She believed in keeping all of the commandments and did so, often at a loss to herself. She believed in "turning the other cheek," as far as possible. As children, we sometimes found this pretty rigid and irksome, but Mother was patient and cheerful with us and usually won her point. I do not remember ever seeing Mother cry or laugh out loud, although she had a great sense of humor. As we became older we could understand why.

Finally the spring of 1888 came, so much to do and so little to do with. Neighbors and relatives often helped each other, but each had a big row to hoe. Now their ingenuity was taxed to the limit, but little by little they managed to forge ahead. There was that long distance from town, the men would often walk, carrying their scant provisions on their backs, stopping to rest along the road at some little farm home.

Father was very good at carpentry and made many useful items for the homes: a drop leaf table, cupboard, even a folding bed for the boys and many other useful items. He also made a sled and many other articles around the farm. He helped the neighbors fix and remodel their homes. He and Mr. Rudine even made caskets for some neighbors, as it was almost impossible to go to town in winter.

Then there was the fuel problem. Mother missed all the wood piles found everywhere to which she had been accustomed. About all that we had at this time was coarse slough hay, cut with a scythe, which had to be twisted and fed with great care because there were no chimneys in most homes. Only a stove pipe came up through the roof. Later a very little soft coal could be purchased.

There wasn't any or very little of the so much publicized "Buffalo coal" to be found. As the little herd of cattle increased this problem was solved with much work and some complaints. There were the straw burners that set on the stove which made a hot fire but also a lot of smoke. Corn was grown, which furnished cobs.

It was only by great economy and thrift and self-denial during the first years that homes were established. So many unforeseen problems and very little or no income, with many more expenses. It became necessary to borrow a little money, often paying as much as ten to twelve percent interest, in order to purchase more oxen and some machinery. Mother and Father would never at any time mortgage the home. They now had two yoke of oxen, three or four cows, a pig or two and some chickens. Milk went a long ways toward furnishing food for the family. They missed the many berries and fruits which grew wild in their native land, especially wild strawberries, blueberries and lingnon berries and also the many lakes where fish was so abundant. When Mother would worry about meat, Father would take his shotgun and bring in a fat rabbit or a duck, sometimes wild geese or even a crane in the spring and fall or an elusive prairie chicken or two. Being a good hunter he generally dressed his game before bringing it in, which Mother appreciated. We children were very much interested when he loaded his gun. He purchased the empty shells, shot, powder and copper caps, and would use some newspaper for packing. Each item was carefully measured and packed into the shell.

The neighbors usually exchanged help when butchering, as the huge barrel of scalding water was used in preparing pork. Mother would make up a great deal of the best sausage imaginable, five or six varieties besides the usual head cheese. That involved a great deal of work. She was very particular about each item and she received many compliments on her sausages and meat preparations. She showed many neighbors how to prepare them. In those days there was the pork barrel for curing meat. Father also had a smokehouse where he used cobs, together with a little hickory or other wood, which he secured from Gus Gerhardt's Lumber Yard in Highmore. Sometimes a little beef was cured and dried, which was very tasty. Mother was also known for her good bread, of which she baked many varieties, white, rye, graham, Swedish Limpa and various rolls for certain occasions, especially at Christmastime.

Later, when milk became more plentiful, she also made cheeses for family use. It was made from sweet, whole milk, which included the cream with rennet added. The most difficult part of that was in the proper pressing and curing. Sometimes she would add anise, caraway seeds, cardamon, and cumin seed, of which Father was very fond. When he was too busy, she sometimes walked two and one-half miles to "Uncle's" place for the early morning milk, carrying the two five gallon pails, this meant a five mile trip. And as the cheese had to be made while the milk was sweet, this made a very strenuous day.

That winter, 1888, which is known as one of the worst in history, many were caught with little food. Some people were out of food and borrowed from neighbors. We heard of people freezing to death also. One woman in Spring Lake Township froze to death in a blizzard.

That spring Henry was six and was sent to school with only a slate and a pencil. The teacher was a Miss Susie Swift. There were about twenty-eight pupils, many of whom were grown boys. Teaching in those days was a tremendous task, requiring plenty of tact and ingenuity. The salary was from $18 to $20 a month or less. Everyone furnished his own books and supplies, which meant a variety of almost nothing. Within a few years there was a movement for the betterment of schools, requiring the uniformity of equipment.

At first Henry learned all the letters of the alphabet, numbers and many words, as well as spelling, from an almanac which belonged to Miss Swift. She said that his progress was very good. It must have been a good beginning as he graduated from the eighth grade at the head of the class; he later taught school himself. As for the health of the school children, except for the usual colds, chill blains and sore throats, all was well. Another early teacher was Mrs. Ed Pettys, who with her aged mother and small children and one baby, occupied the old Sedgwick house, which was now vacated since the Sedgwicks had gone back East. She would go home at noon, one mile from the school house, to care for the baby, leaving instructions with the school children to resume their studies at the proper time until she returned, many times at two o'clock. Needless to say, pandemonium reigned in the meantime.

A school term was usually six months long, three in the fall and three in the spring. Those early teachers must have done a good job, for from this early school came many teachers, an editor and publisher, an attorney, religious and educational leaders and successful farmers, ranchers and businessmen.

Mother was very particular about school attendance. We children were never absent or tardy without a good reason. We walked one and one-half miles to school. Learning the English language was not too difficult for adults as all children in the neighborhood learned it fast and well; they spoke it more fluently than the mother tongue. In Sweden, education was compulsory, and as the children talked English at home, their parents soon learned it as well. It was more easily understood than spoken; many a good laugh was had at the misuse of words, but no one was offended. These laughs were mutual among all of the neighbors.

At this time, Mother and Father subscribed for the Chicago *Bladet,* a weekly paper, which gave the national, international and state news in the Swedish language; later English papers came, including the Hyde County *Bulletin.* As Mother was busy in the evening with many things, Father would read the paper aloud and they would often discuss certain news item.

Often some neighbor would drop in, in the evening, visiting until a late hour. Then worrying a bit about finding the way home, they would locate the North Star as a guide and go on from there. Mother would place the little kerosene lamp in the window as an added precaution. The popular means of motivation in those days was on foot, often many miles, but as they were accustomed to that, it caused no worry.

On still evenings it was possible to tell just who of the neighbors was coming, or who was coming from town, or just how far away they were, by the particular rattle of the wagon or the clank of the harness or by the wheels bumping certain rocks. On dark evenings our little lamp was set in the window so that it could be seen from the road. In the cool of the evening, one could hear the neighbors urging their tired oxen on as they worked them until dark, trying to get their farming done.

The settlers, having heard about many Indian massacres in the earlier territorial days and about Custer's Last Stand, were still very much afraid of possible Indian outbreaks. Many times false alarms came in of Indians being on the rampage, most of which were groundless. The last scare came one day in the fall, a couple years after statehood, and people hastily picked up a few possessions, (whatever food was available), watered their few head of cattle and hastily gathered at a place known as the Nelson farm, two miles east, where there was good water. The women and children were placed in a few wagons and with a few men went to Highmore. Other men stayed behind to care for the livestock. Many people found lodging in an old building that was used as a court house, where they slept on the floor. Soon it was learned that the alarm was partly false. There were many reports. Some Indians had crossed the Missouri River at the Little Bend, the river being very low, and went to a reservation in North Dakota to visit another tribe. These were friendly Indians and later they returned to the Black Hills. It was a great relief when the people heard that they never came this way and all returned home glad to find everything safe.

The next year a small scare occurred in our immediate neighborhood one evening. A partly blind ox meandered around and fell into a shallow well. By the time help was summoned it was dark and a bonfire was built in order to furnish light enabling them to see in getting him out. The neighbors thinking that the Indians were burning us out, caused no little stir, and many cautiously came scouting around to check on the situation. The relief was so great that the poor ox was almost forgotten.

Later, in the early summers, many wagon loads of Indians from the Fort Thompson area would go North, often stopping at some farm home for water and for provisions to stop over night. Sometimes they would ask for bread or milk or some other food to tide them over. They seemed very grateful for any favors. They were very friendly and we were never afraid of them. It was interesting visiting their camp where they pitched their tents. They would arrange their wagons in a little circle around two or three tents. The squaws would dig wild turnips for food of which there were plenty in the spring. There were many children as well as ponies and dogs. At one time we gave them a puppy dog at which they grinned broadly. Sometimes they would want to trade a pony for a lump jaw steer or cow of which there were quite a few at one time. Then they would stay several days, dress the beef, cut it up and dry it before leaving. This would usually be in the early fall on their return back to Fort Thompson. At one time my brothers bought a pony from them for $10.00. We used him for herding cattle for many years.

There were also gypsy bands, which nobody liked, usually four or five wagon loads of swarthy men, women, children, dogs, and ponies. The women would tell fortunes and the men were good horse traders. One day as a gypsy woman called at the door, begging for food or money, another gypsy slipped past Mother into the house, Mother grabbed the broom and out went the gypsy and did not return.

Mother was a small woman but with plenty of grit. Mother was not quite five foot, who weighed 145 pounds. Her eyes were blue, her hair nut brown and was parted in the middle, slightly elevated at the sides and braided into two braids that were coiled at the back of the neck. She carried herself well, very erect at all times. She had a fair complexion and dimples.

The gypsies always had a sick woman and baby in the camp, so they usually begged for a chicken or other food, that being their stock in trade.

Then there was the junk collector at least once each year, with an old wagon and a poor team of horses, sometimes only one horse, who, for a small amount of money, bought old rubber, copper, tin and bones. The children of the neighborhood usually had a pile ready, waiting for his coming, as they were permitted to sell the junk and keep the money. One of these old junk men was very friendly and the children liked him very much, he was known as "Old Kirkendall".

The most interesting of all as far as children were concerned was the early peddler with his huge pack on the back. Sometimes on foot, but usually with a Democrat wagon and thin horse. Most of these peddlers were Syrians or Hungarians and they were expert salesmen. Their packs consisted of many bright and useful articles, such as: dress goods; table cloths; woolen shawls; children's clothing; some brightly colored silken or satin articles; jewelry, gay and pretty of the ten cent variety, which needless to say appealed greatly to the children; and sometimes a little gift was tossed to the youngest member of the family. It was really a little traveling dry goods store, at a selling price. Children were very curious as to the contents of the pack.

One afternoon a cowboy rode in—big hat, chaps, spurs, leather cuffs, boots, bandana, fancy saddle, blanket and bridle. What a thrill that was, for it was awesome and frightened us younger children so that we hid behind Mother's voluminous skirts. A wonderful place to hide at times. He finally coaxed us to come to sit on his lap by giving us either a nickel or a dime. He came for an ox which Father had sold and after spending the night he returned home.

Dakota Territory had become a state in 1889. Four years later we were naturalized citizens, having secured our citizenship papers. We had also made final proof on the homestead. As the children were growing up, Mother said we must have more room. So a two-story house was purchased near Holabird. With the help of neighbors it was moved in the fall of 1897 and placed north of the sod house. It was in fair shape, but winter set in early so it was boarded up until spring.

That year a well was bored, but with no appreciable amount of water, so it was abandoned as it was too crooked to curb. "Uncle Bern" was very good at witching for water, having located several good wells in the neighborhood and one for himself. He found a very good vein about the center of the homestead, so another well was bored the next year which was very good.

That spring, one sultry afternoon the second of May about 4:30, a few thunderheads were forming in the southwestern sky and in no time at all we noticed a very black funnel coming. Father and two of the children just managed to reach the house when it struck full force ripping a long strip off the roof of the house allowing rain and hail to pour in. One south window blew in. Father held the kitchen door with all his might which seemed to bend like a rainbow at both ends. Thunder and lightning seemed to play right on the roof. All fury seemed to break loose; in a few minutes all was over. The frame house was gone, nothing left but a battered side wall lying on the west side of the sod house which luckily was still standing. Everything inside was water soaked and plastered with mud, including the members of the family. The granary was turned over, the barn was not damaged where two boys were, and one was out in the pasture thoroughly soaked, having held on to the hayrake. Luckily no one was injured. There were shingles and splintered wood everywhere for miles around, some stuck two feet into the ground. There was much hail and snow also.

The next day was warm and sunny. Mother and Father were busy all day trying to clean up and dry bedding and clothing. They then decided to buy another house, so Father bought two about ten miles away. One of the neighbors needed one, so in his neighborly manner he sold one to him. This house was moved to the site of the new well in the middle of the quarter. It was repaired somewhat and the family moved into it in the fall. A good basement had been dug for the house and a barn was also erected at this site. The next year another small house was purchased and moved in beside this one and was used for the boys' bedroom. A stock tank was built and later a granary and other improvements were made.

There were dry years, the grass and grain fields dried up in early summer, but the Russian Thistles grew fast and it was a good thing as the cows ate them eagerly and it kept them from drying up. Water was scarce and the cows were often thirsty. The herds of many mixed breeds had increased rapidly and milking and butter-making became a means of livelihood. But markets were poor, and at first, cattle were very cheap. Eggs at one time sold for three cents a dozen and butter at five cents per pound. It spoiled at the stores; some even tried greasing their wagons with it!

Horses had now replaced oxen and the era of the "barefoot boy and girl" became a memory, though with some regrets. In spite of burning ground, cactus, prickly pears, and bloody toes from hard rocks, it had been a pleasure after a scanty shower. When Father became discouraged, watching those promising blue clouds fade away into thin air day after day, Mother would say, "Let's look on the brighter side, and live one day at the time."

She was always busy cleaning, cooking, baking, carding wool, spinning, knitting, mending, making soap, washing and, like other mothers rearing the children, sometimes helping the mothers with their babies as well.

On rare occasions when it became hot and dusty she would say, "It would be nice in Sweden now, no dust or destructive winds – and May Day – what a happy time that was! Everyone dancing in the streets, everyone celebrated May Day. And she hoped to see the midnight sun there again sometime. But there were many good things here, too.

She seldom went to town as she feared leaving the children at home and the trip was long and tiresome. But Father was a good shopper.

He had hated to dispose of a large, long-legged, horned, rather unmanageable brute of an ox, which he had trained to drive single, with the lines over the horns like a horse, on a two-wheeled cart with a large box and spring seat. Starting at dawn in the summertime, we would be in town by nine o'clock.

This was the era of the old fashioned store with the pot-bellied stove which warmed everyone. There were the oatmeal and cracker barrels; Big Fat Cat syrup in wooden ten and fifteen gallon kegs; apple barrels; Tom and Jerry tobacco; Arbuckles, Lion and 4X coffee in paper bags and fifteen and twenty-five cents a pound. Mother bought green coffee and roasted it herself, grinding it on a little coffee mill. Across the street was the "Go to Grassmucks" sign on a little store. It was remarkable what a large line of good things these stores carried! Usually after a lunch of crackers and cheese (mostly free) at McLaughlin's and always a bag of good candy for the kids and a ring of good baloney at the meat shop, it was time to start home, generally about two o'clock. This ox would run nearly all the way like a horse and if the sun was getting low, he would almost become unmanageable, even galloping. Father would do his best to hold him down for fear of overheating. We were home by sundown or after!

Once Mother sheared seven sheep for a neighbor and this lady sewed dresses for us girls in return. She had a sewing machine which we later purchased when they moved back to New York. It was an old Singer and we used it many years. Mother also got some of the wool that she sheared.

August, now aged ten, became quite a hero, having saved the life of a seven year old neighbor boy. As the boys had been sent to get a barrel of water from a well two and one-half miles away, the younger boy crashed through the rotten wood cover into about twenty feet of water. Yelling at him to hold onto the old wooden pump pipe with all his might, then taking the lines from the harness, he made a loop and leaning down on this platform, pulled him out. This worried the mothers a lot and it was decided in the neighborhood to fill a lot of the old abandoned wells and make the others safe. August was given a twenty-five cent reward. Mother had no favorites but August was much more thoughtful of her around the house; he sometimes would give her a nice gift, which the rest of the children hadn't thought of.

We were now one-half mile further from the schoolhouse, which was used for church services, as well as educational and recreational purposes, programs, Lyceum, Literary Society meetings (including debates), basket socials, and Women's Christian Temperance Union, in which there was a good membership for many years. An organ was purchased which added much to the enjoyment. Singing was greatly enjoyed by all at all times; it made up a large part of all entertainment. Elections and public meetings were held there. Church services were conducted regularly on every Lord's Day and everyone attended, coming for many miles. Christmas programs were outstanding.

There was also a Ladies Aid as early as 1892. Sedgwick never lacked in spiritual and moral leadership, which made our community strong and attracted many to the community activities. There were parties for all young people in the homes, with games, lunch and singing around the organ. Some played guitars, and one performer played a zither harp, a harmonica, and foot chimes all at once. There was also dancing in the vicinity, with two or three good fiddlers and sometimes accordionists.

Mother stood for temperance and the WCTU; Carry Nation's activities were justified. The woman suffrage movement now came up, a step in the right direction, but she did not see any need for a woman president. Occasionally a temperance lecturer came. One had a small phonograph and three cylinder records: "Where is My Wandering Boy Tonight?", "Tell Mother I'll Be There," and "In the Sweet By and By". This was a high spot, being the first phonograph here; sometimes he consented to play them over several times. This attracted immense crowds and called for repeat performances.

The Fourth of July was an important holiday now, leaving no question in anyone's mind as to its significance, after listening to a long lecture or sermon and patriotic singing. Picnics followed.

In the spring of 1897, a 500 pound capacity cream separator was purchased, also a forty gallon churn, which was turned by hand. Father had constructed a new dairy room which led into the very cold basement. It was well screened. Mother and Father decided to milk thirty-two cows, with the help of the children. Butter could be shipped into Chicago at low rates and for good prices, nineteen cents being tops. During the summer 100 pounds of butter per week were shipped in forty and sixty pound wooden tubs. Some of our neighbors milked as many as forty-five cows. This was an endless, back-breaking job; washing and sterilizing all the equipment, carrying cream and buttermilk up and down the basement stairs and out to feed the calves and chickens. The price of hogs was very low, there were few raised. Buttermilk was at a premium, we even had a team of horses which drank a pail of buttermilk apiece a day.

What a blessing it was, when later a creamery was started in Highmore, this did away with so much drudgery.

In this summer of 1897 everything moved along smoothly until the Fourth of July, which found a lot of the neighboring children in bed with the measles, including two of us, in a few days all five. (The real thing!) The weather was torrid and so were the measles, not much air with the windows darkened. Poor Mother! Trying to care for the sick and helping Father milk those thirty-two cows all in full production. Caring for the milking utensils was a tremendous task. Father must have milked the clock around! How they fed all those calves and everything, we'll never understand. Soon two of the boys were able to help, but we all came out quite weak for sometime afterwards. The temperature was 90 and 100 degrees and did its best.

Herds of cattle and horses increased by huge numbers. It became difficult to keep them from trespassing; friendships were sometimes strained. Peace prevailed, however, and fencing became a necessity. More range and hayland became necessary. Horse production had become more profitable than cattle. An open grazing period was permitted during the winter months; hundreds of horses grazed on the open range all winter making it imperative that everyone protect their own interests.

There were new things coming into the home at this time: a new malleable [iron] Home Comfort Range replacing the old cast iron stove, a new sitting room sofa, and other items. This was the time of the hard coal heater, gas lamps, carpeted floors, parlor stand with the plush covered family album, Nottingham lace curtains, and also the mantle kerosene lamp with its large bowl painted with beautiful red roses, the stereoscope with its views; everyone felt that they were making great strides in progress.

This was the beginning of a boom period, having much more rain, better crops, showing the richness of the new soil; there were better markets, and many improvements. Horse drawn headers, riding plows, discs, larger harrows, some binders, and that very wonderful machine, the horse powered threshing machine! This meant quite a crew making a great deal of extra work for the housewives. Mother cooked and baked and cleaned for days. The neighbors borrowed extra dishes from each other. Sometimes many men stayed overnight, making more meals. We children looked forward to threshing, what activity and excitement! There were now larger hay mowers, rakes and loaders. In the early morning, especially in the spring, one man was kept busy caring for the work horses, feeding, grooming, harnessing six or seven teams before breakfast, often before daylight. Those days were long. Many times it was midnight before bedtime. These were all hard days for Mother.

With all this activity, Father found the time to go out and do extra carpentry, which brought in extra income. There were now cattle to sell. The boys delivered them cowboy style, taking them to either Lebanon, Highmore or Gettysburg. This was a big job.

In the spring of 1904 people began planting trees. Mother was a bit doubtful, but Father, with the help of a neighbor, John Bitney, planted a lot of trees. Some were six and seven feet tall, including: ash, cottonwood, poplar, two fir and spruce, plums, currant and gooseberry bushes, twenty-five apple trees, even strawberries. They grew fast and lived until the grasshopper and dust bowl period of the thirties, all except the apple trees.

This was in early April, but Father did not live to enjoy the fruits of his labor. He became chilled in a wet snow shower while riding horseback, which developed into pneumonia that night. A young doctor was called, and said that progress was good. Father suddenly died, May 18, 1904. We were stunned, he was only fifty-four years old. He was always strong and healthy, busy and ambitious, particular of his personal appearance at all times. We had not thought it could happen to him, being very capable at everything, also holding township offices of various kinds. Mother, as always, was calm and composed, a marvelous example of fortitude for the family.

Now it was necessary for the boys to take over and carry on as before. The eldest was twenty-one. Mother's health suffered and though not complaining it became necessary for her to rest more.

The next year the boys purchased a steam-run threshing rig and together with some neighbor boys put in a very good run of threshing. It required quite a crew, as one hauled water in two large tanks; as straw was used for heat, one man was fireman, then there was the feeder and the boss. Mother worried a great deal as all three boys were gone all fall.

Now came the land boom, with many new settlers from Illinois, Iowa, Nebraska, and Minnesota moving into Hyde County. Many of them built new homes. It was said that at one time there were some forty real estate dealers in the county.

During these better years some of the hardships were forgotten, the hard winters, prairie fires, droughts, and even the open winters with their sharp, icy gales.

This was the time for the last struggle between Pierre and Mitchell for the honor of the state capitol of South Dakota. It was a great six day event and nearly everyone attended, all of us except Mother, her health not permitting. There were huge crowds. Everything was free: railroad fares, buttons, lunches, noise makers and all. There were songs, speeches, parades, brass bands, even free boat rides on the

Missouri. To the younger generation it was a wonderful experience, being the first of its kind here. Pierre was the winner, becoming the permanent state capitol.

There were many more improvements at this time, among them: the surrey and the top buggy, fancy harness, high stepping buggy teams, gaily colored cord fly nets with bright tassels, driving gloves, fancy buggy whips, and beautiful lap robes. The horses were sleek and shiny from careful grooming; manes trimmed, tails braided and tied with a red ribbon, fancy bridle and check rein. Ah! this was the ultimate in style! The young men of the community had excellent saddle horses with good saddles but very few spurs.

How can anyone forget those long, sweeping flared skirts, leg-o'-mutton sleeves, high collars, high button shoes(needletoe), black cotton hose, "merry widow" hats with large plumes, ribbons or flowers, and ten to twelve inch hat pins. And "my Lady's hour-glass" figure (curves in the right places by various aids) and tremendous "hair dos".

For the men—black "plug" hats, celluloid collars, stiff shirt fronts or white dickeys, button shoes, handlebar mustaches or beards (sometimes a Van Dyke), vest and massive gold watch chain and charm, rather close fitting pants and, for the younger boys, knee pants, ruffled white blouse, and long black stockings.

Mother liked nice clothes, her tastes were modest and conservative. There had been few during these difficult years. She did not approve of the corset or bustle.

We girls had now purchased a new piano. Emma was taking music lessons while I was teaching school. Henry had taught three terms of school by this time, and was also township clerk. August did hold, and still holds, township offices.

With so many activities coming up: the church movement, artesian well digging, building of the telephone lines, boys threshing, young people coming and going a great deal, perhaps we did not notice that Mother had to spend more time in bed with sleepless nights. Though young Dr. Burnside attended her several times, she did not improve. She would rally and spend a great deal of time outdoors, usually in the garden.

Several years before, Mother had had a very serious illness and had lapsed into a state of coma for some time. This was due to weakness from loss of blood. It was thought that she was dead. The young doctor said that nothing could be done. But for some miraculous reason she slowly recovered. Later she said that, being unable to move, but hearing faint voices speaking of death and funerals, she became frightened that she might be buried alive, and with great effort managed to move her lips a bit, whereupon she was given a few drops of water. After this she really never regained her strength but managed quite well.

What wonderful strides the medical profession has made since those days! Her ambitious spirit was handicapped by lack of endurance and she felt a bit disappointed at times.

One day in the summer of 1907, Mother received word from Sweden that her uncle, Arvid Arvidson, had died and shortly afterward that her mother, too, had passed away at the age of ninety. Mother was somewhat depressed and said that she would have liked to see them so much!!

In the winter of 1907, the Sedgwick Telephone Company was formed; its construction went forward the next year. Everyone looked forward to this. Henry was secretary-treasurer of the corporation; the business meetings were held in the homes, including ours.

That year also, it was a certainty that the Sedgwick church would be built, which came about in 1908. Mother had managed to attend the meetings. Mother had voted for the new church and had become a charter member.

It now became necessary for people to increase their water supply, so we decided to drill an artesian well. One day in early October the boys were at the neighbor's helping to bring the well drillers to our place. Mother had spent a few days in bed and this afternoon she awoke; her eyes bright and her face flushed and with a little smile, asked for a drink of water. Then she said quietly in her usual thoughtful manner, "Maybe you had better have "Aunty Bern" come over, and tell the boys to come home." That was all, but somehow we understood and she quietly slipped away about 10:30, peacefully and quietly as she had lived, on October 4, 1907.

Without boasting in any manner I would like to accord to the memory of our Mother the honor due her for her integrity and her religious way of life, which contributed in a measure to the good of the community.

Mother was often very quiet and talked very little of the past, only when some of her friends would tease her a bit. She would say that she married Father for his good character and that America was fine, a wonderful place for boys especially, to grow up in, no compulsory military obligations here as in Europe, no snobby aristocrats, everyone was friendly and good and what wonderful freedom and liberty!

by Huldah Johnson Simonette, daughter

# Mathilda Andersdotter Berg
## Grant County
## 1881

Mathilda was born in Skaraborgslan, Vestergotland, Sweden in 1854. In 1878 she married Carl Berg. Times in Sweden were hard and though the poorer people labored day and night, they had very little income to support their families. Hearing reports from relatives who had immigrated to America, Mr. and Mrs. Berg became interested in this country. Seeking a better way of living, they decided to go to America. In May, 1881, Carl and Mathilda Berg and their little daughter, Hilda Elizabeth, took all their earthly belongings and boarded the steamship "Arizona," leaving their native land to seek their fortune in America.

After docking in New York, they went by train to Dakota Territory. The train ran only as far as Big Stone City because of a wash-out in the grade, so the railroad hired a drayman to take them and their trunks to Milbank. Their goal was to reach Andrew Berg's place (Carl's brother) which was a homestead near what is now Stockholm.

From Milbank, they walked a distance of about ten and a half miles. The next day they came to the Sundin place where Carl's brother Andrew was staying. Soon Carl (whose name became Charles in America) filed for a free homestead.

They built a small, two-room, wooden frame house on the homestead in the fall of 1881 and moved into it in March, 1882. They had a cookstove and a table, chairs, and beds with straw mattresses. The furniture was all made by Mr. Berg. One of the beds had a telescopic arrangement and could be folded back during the day to make the house roomier. They made a barn by digging into the side of a ravine and covered the roof with hay and tree boughs.

Charles Arthur, born in 1882, was the first white child to be born in Stockholm township.

Mr. and Mrs. Berg were almost the only settlers around who owned a team of oxen, which they called Tom and Dick.

These beasts of burden were used to plow, drag and seed the fields. They also purchased two cows, and during the summer these cows and the neighbors' cows were herded together in a common herd. When Arthur became old enough, his job was to herd these cows out in the open prairie. There were Indians living in the nearby ravines and although they were peaceable, Mrs. Berg was always frightened when they would come to the door and want to trade something for some of her freshly baked bread or other food staples.

Pioneer days on the early homesteads were filled with many hardships and long hours filled with toil and hard physical labor. Mrs. Berg would walk from the homestead near Stockholm, to Milbank, carrying butter, which she had made, to exchange for sugar, coffee and other needed items. Of course, Mr. Berg walked to Milbank after needed items many times, also.

The first year they farmed, someone was hired to cut the grain but it had to be tied in bundles by hand. In 1887, Mr. Berg and his brother, August, went together and purchased a six-foot binder. Although this machine had no bundle carrier, it was a great improvement over tying the bundles by hand.

Charles and Mathilda Berg now had a family of eight children. A large supply of "vittles" was necessary to keep a family of this size fed. The diet included potatoes, bread, milk, pancakes, grot (rice and oatmeal) and home-butchered and cured salt pork. The meat had to be canned or cured as there was no means of refrigeration in those days. Electricity was not available in the Stockholm area until 1924.

Religion and worship of God was not an area which was neglected in the lives of this family. They attended a Sunday School held by the Covenant denomination. When there were no churches to attend, the pioneer families met in private homes or in the school houses for worship. After the Lutheran church was built in Strandburg, the Berg family attended services there.

The children attended a one-room school house where they learned their "three r's" as well as the English language. School was held for only two months in the fall and two months in the spring. During the cold winter months and stormy weather, school was dismissed. Going to school only four months out of a year prohibited the students from progressing very far in one year.

In 1898, Mr. Berg's health began failing and he was unable to work. In 1899 he passed away at the age of forty-five years, leaving his wife with the large family to care for and raise.

The aim of Mrs. Berg's life was to get out of debt. With the help of her sons, this goal was accomplished one day in September. When the boys finished threshing, they figured out they could pay their Uncle August the $400 which they owed him. The family was now debt-free and this was a big burden off the mind of Mrs. Berg. Three days later, she lay down for a nap, a nap from which she never awoke. After a life of toil and hardship, Mathilda (Anderson) Berg died in 1916 at the age of sixty-two.

Although small of stature, she gave much encouragement and help to her family after the early death of her husband. We wonder how she found the strength and time to do the many tasks required in the family's struggle to survive. In talking to relatives it was reported that Mrs. Berg was a God-fearing woman and turned to Him for help and guidance in raising her family.

# THE LONE DANE

Marie Christensen Johnson
Clay County
1870

Mother was born in Hostrup, Denmark on May 22, 1842 and baptized Marie Christensen. On the day of her confirmation she stood at the foot of her class; at the head stood a small, white-haired lad with too-large hands and feet and a rather prominent nose. His name was Charles Johnson. Mother worked as a goose girl, nursemaid, house maid and dairy maid until she was twenty-eight years old when she again met Charles Johnson, just returned from America after working three years on the Union Pacific Railroad just completed. At a dance he asked Marie to go with him to America and become his wife. She consented, although some of the older women cautioned her that he might even sell her to a Black man, but Marie had no fear.

On April 12, 1870 the young engaged couple and a small party of friends left Copenhagen on the emigrant ship "Ocean Queen" and at the end of nineteen days arrived in New York. To her great dismay Mother found that her chest containing all her earthly possessions had failed to be put on board ship. A trunk belonging to Peter Jorgenson, a member of the party, was also missing. At a consultation it was decided that mother and Peter Jorgenson were to remain until their baggage came. Father and the rest of the party were to go on to Dakota Territory. Mother found work at Smith's emigrant home and at the end of three weeks the missing baggage arrived, but they were to pay fifty dollars to get it. This was a calamity since the two only had fifty-five dollars between them. However, the emigrant home allowed Mother to pack a large hamper of food for the trip to Dakota Territory.

In the meantime father had filed on a claim relinquished by a young homesteader. The claim was in Clay County, thirteen miles northwest of what is now Vermillion. He was at the Sioux City depot waiting for Mother and Mr. Jorgenson when they arrived. Roads were muddy and but a trail, so the first day they traveled only twenty miles. They spent the first night at the home of an Indian.

Here they purchased two cows and tied them behind their wagon. From then on Mother and Mr. Jorgenson took turns walking the last twenty-five miles and prodding the cows; neither dared to drive. When at dusk they arrived at a small log cabin, their new home, a black dog named "June" ran out to greet them and to lick their hands.

Next morning Mother took inventory of her new home: one room, one window, one door, sod roof and floor. There was one kettle, one frying pan and a coffee pot. She also found two plates, two cups and saucers, two knives and forks. There was an old stove, a bed and table made of rough lumber and a bench.

Their first day was spent in walking to Rev. Christensen's homestead, two miles south, to be married. Here also was but one room and in order not to embarrass the young couple, Rev. Christensen went outside to remove his coat while he put on his robe and collar. They walked back again as husband and wife and near their door stood the red cow named "Squaw," licking a new calf. "Our wedding gift, Marie," said father.

That first winter father spent a good deal of his time in felling trees that grew along the Missouri river. The logs were for a new house. They also needed fuel. One day while Mother was alone she heard June making an unusual lot of noise. Mother was just going to open the door when it was opened from without. Here stood two young Indians with hunting knives, a gun, and spattered with blood. Mother was frightened but she neither screamed nor fainted. June stood at her side. One Indian handed her a paper from his pocket. She looked it over, nodded as if she understood. She could not read a word—nor could he. They then motioned for something to eat. She gave them bread and coffee. The Indians then wanted flour and salt which she also gave them, hoping they would leave, which they did. Then one returned carrying the heart and liver of an antelope in his hands. These he deposited on the table. Mother's fright vanished when she saw the reason for their blood-spattered clothing. They had shot and dressed an antelope.

That same fall came other guests in the form of a flock of geese. On their way south they were stopping to feed in a nearby field where oats had been harvested. Father was a good shot and had a good gun but not one bullet. This was a calamity. Mother had brought along a clock carefully wrapped in a feather tick but in spite of all the pains she had taken to keep it in good condition it refused to tick-tick in this new land. The pendulum had two heavy weights of lead. Of these they made bullets. When everything was ready, Father took a horse that he knew did not fear shooting and walked alongside of it close to the geese. He pulled the trigger and when the smoke cleared there lay seven geese.

Mother's next home was also log, much like the first but larger and it had a "lean-to" for a bedroom. It also had a board floor and shingle roof, a great improvement. Now they did not have to sit on the bed under an umbrella during a rain. In this house ten of her eleven children were born. In 1878, just eight years after they located, they built a large brick barn which still stands. All the brick were made and burned on the farm. They were planning to build a brick house in the near future, then came the flood of 1881. However, the brick house was built in due time.

Of her eleven children, eight lived to grow up. Marie Johnson lived to be ninety-eight years old. She never went back to her native Denmark, nor did she wish to. America had given her a good home and she never forgot how seasick she had been on the emigrant ship "Ocean Queen."

Mr. and Mrs. Charles Johnson are buried in the Danish-Lutheran Cemetery south of Gayville, South Dakota just one mile from their original homestead home.

Written by Mrs. Chris Sorenson, daughter of the Charles Johnsons

# MIDWIVES AND A DOCTOR

## Christina Welsz Warnke
## Hutchinson County
## 1877

Christina was born in South Russia in 1849, of German stock. At the age of nineteen she was married to Christoph Warnke, and they came to America with their three children in 1877. At this time the young mother was twenty-eight. The family home was established three miles east of what is now Tripp. Four more children were born in this country.

At that time the nearest place for the pioneer families to do any buying was Yankton, which was reached only after a tedious journey of approximately three days, either on foot or with the patient ox teams. This meant that many times the mother had to be alone for at least a week until the man of the family returned, and at that time many a hostile Indian was roaming the plains.

During these childbearing years and for many years after, Mrs. Warnke was the midwife for many miles in all directions and never a storm was too severe or roads too bad for this indomitable little woman to set forth and give of her help and knowledge to ease the pangs of birth for other pioneer women. Conditions in most of the homes she entered were far from ideal and many times she had to furnish clothing and prepare food for the family in addition to her duties as midwife. She got little or no pay for her work in many instances but was always ready to go when called.

In 1894 the family moved into the new town of Tripp and their home was always a gathering place for old and young. It is a well known fact in this community that Mrs. Warnke delivered over 3000 babies and she was usually able to remember them when she met them on the street throughout the years. Naturally as time went on medical doctors came and she encountered much opposition from them. The older families on the farms remained loyal to her and many of them took advantage of the fact that she was not allowed to make set charges for her work and in this manner many exploited her kindness. She was never able to turn anyone away that came to her.

She was throughout all of her long life bubbling over with jokes and good humor and just having her around was a good tonic for the sick. We feel that she truly practiced to the fullest extent the life of a good neighbor and did all this during the very hardest times experienced by the early pioneers.

Submitted by Ella Nuss, Chair, Pioneer Daughters, Tripp Study Club

\* \* \*

## Martha Habersdotter Johnson Tisdall
## Walworth County
## 1886

Martha Habersdotter was born in Bergen, Norway, in 1833, one of a large family of brothers and sisters. Early in life she developed the aptitude for the care of the sick that was to carry her from her native Norway, first to Wisconsin, then Iowa, and eventually to Dakota Territory.

Trained in the old and honorable Scandinavian profession of midwifery, she fulfilled the tradition of generations of the women in her family. With a little black satchel, the hallmark of her profession as midwife, and still a young girl, she came to Wisconsin just prior to the Civil War.

Then she married a Mr. Johnson, of which union a child, Oliver, was born. Her husband, a soldier in the Civil War, was killed early during the first year of that war.

Joining relatives in Cass County, Iowa, she met and married Johannes Tisdall, a widower with six children. She came with him to Blue Blanket Territory in 1886.

Her fame as a trained midwife spread from her own community to those adjoining. She was many years ahead of her generation in the firm conviction that cleanliness is the first requisite in the care of illness.

Martha Tisdall went about combating age-old superstitions and the sour disapproval of the medical profession.

She substituted clean, hot water for warm chicken blood or weasel skins, for treatment of infections, and boiled water and boiled milk in typhoid cases, clean linen and rigid sanitation for obstetrics. The physicians of her day gave her first grudging acceptance, and finally whole-hearted admiration and respect.

Mrs. Tisdall delivered many babies all alone, often under the most trying circumstances. No one ever asked her help in vain.

She had a congenitally crippled hip, which was a handicap to her. Nevertheless, she carried on.

One time, during the breaking of the ice on the Missouri River, Mrs. Tisdall crossed the river in a row boat to get to her patient. One big Indian rowed the boat, another fended off the swirling chunks of ice that threatened to smash the boat, but she was needed on that other side and she went.

In later years, she became Grandma Tisdall, not alone to her own grandchildren, who are numerous, but to the whole community. She died at the age of 81. She was mother to thirteen children.

\* \* \*

## Anna Marie Weberndoerfer Feistner
## Jerauld County
## 1883

Anna Marie Weberndoerfer was born at Allesheim, province Bavaria, Germany on October 22, 1844. She came to America in 1870, along with her fiance, Pastor Leonard Feistner. She and Pastor Feistner were married at Cedar Falls, Iowa on August 21, 1870.

Pastor Feistner served parishes in Nemaha County, Nebraska and then moved on to Council Bluffs, Iowa for seven years. In 1883 the family moved to homestead on a farm southwest of Woonsocket and Pastor Feistner began missionary work to establish Lutheran churches in the territory.

Anna Marie Weberndoerfer Feistner

Grandma Feistner (as she was known to me) had taken a course in midwifery in Germany and was called upon many times to help in the delivery of babies, and also in many other emergency cases of care of the sick.
Grandmother was the mother of eleven children. She always had a big garden and also sewed all their clothes, including Pastor's suits. She handsewed many, many quilts giving them to her children, and at least one for each grandchild. There were fifty-six grandchildren.

\* \* \*

## Dr. Feige Werner Van Dalse
## Beadle County
## 1889

She was an immigrant girl, born in Saxony, Germany, in 1844. When she was eighteen years of age, she was united in marriage to the Reverend William Feige and the young couple promptly set sail for America.

Before coming to America she had studied medicine, and she had been admitted to the practice of her profession in Germany. When the young couple arrived in America, they first settled at Albany, New York. Shortly thereafter they removed to Missouri, where he preached and she practiced medicine. In the early 1870's, the family removed to Iowa, where he continued to preach and she practiced medicine for ten years. They moved to Dakota Territory in February, 1883 and settled on a homestead ten miles north of Huron.

While living in that vicinity, Dr. Feige practiced her profession roundabout for a period of six years, rendering a large service to the pioneers in that locality. It was her lips that pressed the lips of the new-born babes first when they entered this world, and it was her hands that laid them out when now and then one passed away. She went from home to home, cared for the sick and helped to bury the dead. She was a genuine pioneer doctor – one called to a large service for humanity.

In 1889 the Feiges moved to Huron where she continued the practice of her profession. Her practice grew until within a few years she had the largest practice in Huron. She acquired a great deal of property and soon became one of the wealthiest women in the city.

On one occasion, when five different men doctors had refused to go to a country home where sickness prevailed on account of the severity of the storm which was raging at the time, Dr. Feige made her way to the place and gave relief to a suffering woman. She was possessed of the real pioneer spirit, and no task was to arduous for her to undertake.

# ACCOUNTS OF THE TRIP OVER

## Sophia Hildebrandt Geisler
## Hutchinson County
## 1880

Sophia Hildebrandt was born in Kuhlm, Russia in 1860. Her people were of German descent and were among those who took advantage of the offer of Russian rulers to come to Russia for free land and immunity from military service in exchange for teaching farming methods to the Russians. Her childhood was spent in a large colony where her duties consisted of caring for younger children and helping in the grain fields. Little time was given to the schooling of the children of the colony and the little there was devolved mainly on religious teachings.

Her marriage to Daniel Geisler in March, 1880 meant a severing of family ties in Russia as the honeymoon was spent on the voyage to America. Many relatives had preceded the young couple to this country so they did have the comfort of seeing familiar faces when they came to Dakota.

* * *

## Karolina Mueller Frasch
## Hutchinson County
## 1889

It was the year 1805 that Johann Georg Frasch and family of Wendligen/Nurtingen community of Wurttemberg, Germany, migrated to Crimea, Russia, a peninsula in the Black Sea. Many other German farmers emigrated upon the invitation of Czarina Catherine the Great of Russia during a hundred year period, beginning about 1760. The journey was an arduous overland task, made with an ox or horse cart, carrying their belongings and the younger children, while the adults walked. Nights were spent camping out.

The seventh of their ten children, Freiderich Frasch, married Karolina Mueller. Her family had also migrated to Russia in 1805.

Karolina had twelve brothers and sisters. One, Friederika, came to the U.S.A., and died in Scotland, South Dakota in 1893. Otherwise none of the Frasch or Mueller families immigrated to the United States except Mr. and Mrs. Freiderich Frasch who broke the ties with families and traditions to locate in the Western World. Mr. and Mrs. Freiderich Frasch and eight of their eleven children immigrated to the United States May 11, 1891 (May 23 according to the Russian calendar.) They arrived in Scotland, South Dakota, on June 19.

The family lived in Scotland until August when they moved to a farm east of the James River at Tuscan. The Milwaukee Railroad crossed the James at Tuscan and would stop there for water for the steam locomotive. Mr. Frasch evidently saw the value of the river bottom land when he bought this place. Their youngest child, Bertha, was born on this farm. The older children went to public school part time in order to learn the language.

Written by Naomi Hagstrom Frasch from family records compiled over the years, originally started by Adolph Frasch.

\* \* \*

## Amelia Julia Arneson Hanson
## Union County
## 1875

When Juri Ankerson was a small girl in Norway, her father, a lumberjack, was one of the first to get out to break up a log jam in the spring, when the ice began thawing in the river near their home. His life was lost in this effort.

Juri's mother was left with four children, two boys and two girls. The small family group migrated to the United States. Each family was required to bring with them provisions for the trip. This consisted of one small chest of food. Storms during the trip blew their boat so far off its course that the six week boat trip required thirteen weeks to complete. Because of this, rationing of the food aboard became necessary before they reached their destination. The family finally settled in Allamakee county, the northeastern-most county in Iowa.

It was here that Juri met and married a young wagonmaker from Beloit, Wisconsin, by the name of Arne Arneson. The pioneering spirit led the newlyweds to the new lands in the west. They settled on homestead land in what is now Lincoln County, South Dakota.

They brought their belongings in a covered wagon drawn by an ox and a horse. Arne made the long trek mostly on foot, walking beside his beasts of burden, and in so doing, wore out three pairs of shoes on the trip.

\* \* \*

## Lena Hafstad Westley Gravning
## Deuel County
## 1879

Pioneer women of Dakota Territory were a hardy lot. They must have been strong to endure the hardships they encountered upon coming to this bare, treeless plain. It is a wonder they survived the blizzards in the winter and the heat in the summer. Just imagine coming to a vast prairie with no roads or fences to mark the way. There were no homes to "come home to", because, as yet, no houses had been built. Imagine yourself as a young homemaker with a family coming to such a setting.

This is the situation my grandmother, Lena Hafstad Westley faced in October of 1879, when she and her husband, Eric Westley, came to southern Deuel County in Grange Township. She was twenty-six years old at that time, having been born in 1853 in the province of Telemark, Norway.

She came to America with her parents, Thor and Maria Hafstad and some of her brothers and sisters in 1869. The family settled in Fillmore County, in southern Minnesota, near the towns of Rushford and Peterson. This hilly country bore a strong resemblance to the homeland they had left.

Many of the Norwegian pioneers of Deuel County had at one time lived in Fillmore County.
This young family came here with their three children. A few days after their arrival, another daughter, Inga, was born. A few years later another daughter, Julia (Gurina), was born. The eldest daughter, Mary, had remained in Fillmore County to stay with her grandparents. This seemed to be custom that one child should stay behind to care for the aging grandparents. Two of Lena's sisters had likewise, remained in Norway. I wonder if she realized at that time, in 1879, that she was never to see her daughter Mary again.

We know that when they arrived here, they built a sod house as their first home. They must have built a sod barn too, as they brought a few cattle with them. Nothing much is known about their home furnishings, but I still have the table they brought with them.

It was in April, 1885 that Eric Westley died. Life must have been hard for a widow with five children. She used to tell about driving to Brookings with a team of horses and a load of wheat to have ground into flour.

And so, in 1888, she filed for homestead papers on the northeast quarter of section twelve in Grange Township. That same year, a young bachelor, John (Jon) Gravningen, filed for ownership of the southwest quarter of section six in Blom Township. These two pieces of land cornered each other.

Lena Westley and John Gravning were married sometime before 1889. They made their home on her land in section twelve. John and Lena were the parents of five children. In the spring of 1906, Lena again became a widow. She continued to live on the same farm until her death.

I have often wondered what thoughts went through the minds of these people when they left a homeland, and started out on a journey so strange and unfamiliar to them. I wonder if they ever feared for survival. She had at times said they had nothing to lose, as they were starving to death in Norway. After a few years, Fillmore County became overpopulated, and again they faced the same situations. Here, they did make a living in spite of hardships and sorrows.

Written by her granddaughter, Oreska Gravning Stroschen, February, 1975

# Katrina Adamsen Hansen
# Buffalo County
# 1874

"Trina was nine. She lived on the island of Als, off the coast of Denmark, in a tiny thatched-roofed cottage with her parents. It was her task, while her parents were away working for the big landowner, to take care of her brother Anders, who was three, and to care for the family goat. As she tended to her duties, she used to watch the beautiful billowing clouds as they tumbled in the sky overhead, their shifting white display against the blue sky, making lovely patterns...white sails...drifting beyond the unknown horizon to begin their trek hither and yon...and so she dreamed of the white sails and wondered if some day she would be like them and drift out beyond the horizon...seeking...finding...?"

It is this way Mrs. Inga Hansen Dickerson in her story "Trina" introduces you to her mother who came to America and to Dakota Territory, one of the pioneers who settled Turner County.

"Trina grew to womanhood in the turbulent times around 1864 when the Germans were massing their troops behind the great wall of Dannevirke, the southern border of their beloved Denmark. She met Peder Bursen, a young man from across the channel, who had been forced into the German army after the fall of Dannevirke. He finally secured his release from the army, but knew he could be recalled at any time. Having married Trina, and not wishing to go back to serve the Germans again, he talked her parents and others into going with him and Trina to America."

\* \* \*

Olina Holvick Halseth

## Olina Holvick Halseth
## Lake County
## 1882

At the age of nine years, in 1869, she came with her parents, six brothers and sisters, in a sailboat, to America from Norway. They were on the ocean six or seven weeks, before arriving in New York. She went with her parents to Wisconsin where she lived 'til she was confirmed in the West Prairie Church near Rising Sun.

Upon their arrival in Wisconsin the family had to go out and find work as the family income was very low, being newcomers to this country. Olina, along with some other girls, went to Fargo, North Dakota to find work. She worked as a maid in a Judge's home for several years. Her wage was three dollars a week.

She often spoke of her trip across the ocean and her girlhood days in America. Each family on the boat had their own food which was kept in a wooden chest. This was flat bread, dried beef, and other things easily made from flour. She talked often of the cook house that was fastened to the top of the boat where all the cooking was done. One day a storm came up and blew this off, along with most of their food. They had to make the best of it 'til they got to land. They depended on the wind to bring them over and their boat being a sailboat went with the wind. Some days they'd be blown back as far as they had gone ahead the day before.

\* \* \*

## Anna Raasch Helbring
## Hamlin County
## 1881

Anna Raasch was born in Germany in 1864. At the age of eight she came to the United States. Her family settled in Sauk County, Wisconsin, the nearest town being Abelmans.

In 1879 her father, Frederick Raasch, came to South Dakota and purchased railroad land near Castlewood. He returned to Wisconsin and lack of funds forced him to remain there on his farm until the spring of 1881 at which time he and a daughter, Mary, came to South Dakota. They traveled in a freight car with the stock and machinery, a very scant supply. They stayed with a family named Waltz, who lived on a farm near Mr. Raasch's land.

Anna Raasch arrived in Watertown in May, having made the trip alone on the Northwestern railroad. She recalls that her train ticket had been sewed into her clothes and her embarrassment in producing it for the conductor.

In June her mother and the other six children came in a freight car. They brought the household belongings and one horse which had been injured and couldn't be brought at the time the father came.

Written by Vera A. Helms

\* \* \*

## Thea Anderson Benson
## Deuel County
## 1884

Thea Anderson was born, one of nine girls, many miles from Oslo, Norway, in the year 1855. There among the pine covered hills, she grew up. She gathered lingon berries on the hills, and ran home to drink milk and to eat flat bread baked on top of their stove, as there was no oven.

As Thea grew to womanhood, she worked "out" for $20.00 a year. Her employer gave her enough raw wool to card, spin and to knit into two dresses a year.

At twenty-nine years of age, and in the year 1884, she had saved enough money for passage to America. Her sister, Gena Anderson Olson, and Gena's two daughters and one son had come to Brandt, Dakota Territory, a few years before. In Norway, Gena had left a twenty year old son, and this son came to America with Thea. They came to Ellis Island, on to Chicago, Illinois, and then to Gary in Dakota Territory.

Thea and her nephew were met by no one when they arrived by train at Gary. So they found and sat in a building all day. In the evening, a man came to lock up the building. He spoke Norwegian, and took them to his home for the night. The next day he drove them to Brandt.

By Selma Benson Tietjen

\* \* \*

## Emma Carlson Walsh
## Lincoln County
## 1873

Emma Sophia Carlson was born in Christiania, Norway, May 8, 1872. Father and Mother Carlson with their two small daughters, their son and the nine day-old baby, Emma Sophia, sailed for America May 17, 1872. A Friend had written of opportunities in America. There were kin in the new world but they did not know of their whereabouts until later. In mid-ocean their ship was rammed by another which had gotten off course. Water rushed into the hole made by the impact. People were in a panic. Some screamed, some prayed. Carpenters on board quickly repaired the breakage and the journey proceeded. After four long weeks the ship docked at Ellis Island.

The Carlson family took the first out-going train to Omaha, Nebraska, arriving there in the night. Sleeping quarters were provided in the depot. Father Carlson found employment on the railroad. They soon picked up some English and learned much about Dakota's "Free Land."

Printed in United States of America

**PINE HILL PRESS, INC.**
Freeman, S. Dak. 57029

# Daughters of Dakota

### VOLUME I
From sunbonnets and headbands to babushkas and Paris designer hats, this parade of over half a century of women represents the "Daughters of Dakota." They are all ages, speak a dozen tongues, and come to the territory riding on horseback, in stone boats and even model T's. They come alone, with girlfriends, husbands, parents, or as widows with children. Some are entranced by the haunting beauty of the Dakota prairies; others go mad with loneliness. For all, their new life is a struggle.

**$11.95**

### VOLUME II
"The attic was not history when I was growing up," says the author. "History was the story of men getting mad at each other; who fought when, why, and who won . . . 'the pioneer came west with his wife and his cattle,' I learned in school. This is the attic history of how the pioneer came West with her family and friends."

**$11.95**

### VOLUME III
White women came into Dakota territory with an almost pathological fear of Indians. Those who could conquer their prejudices found unexpected friendship and cooperation with a people they believed were "savage" and "warlike." Where treaties were respected by settlers, peaceful coexistence prevailed. Cultural misunderstandings—many humorous—emerge from the pages of the book, as do stories of cultural sharing.

**$12.95**

---

## ORDER FORM

Name _____

Address _____

City _____

State/Zip _____

**Send Check or Money Order to:**
GFWC of SD/DOD
Box 349, Yankton, SD 57078

Volume I — $11.95 _____

Volume II — $11.95 _____

Volume III — $12.95 _____

Volume IV — $12.95 _____

Shipping & Handing $1.50 per book _____

**TOTAL** $_____